TRANSPLANT
TRIATHLETE

TRANSPLANT
TRIATHLETE
THE STORY OF HOW ONE MAN
WENT FROM ILLNESS TO IRONMAN

DICCON DRIVER

First published by Pitch Publishing, 2016

Pitch Publishing
A2 Yeoman Gate
Yeoman Way
Worthing
Sussex
BN13 3QZ

www.pitchpublishing.co.uk
info@pitchpublishing.co.uk

ISBN 978-1-78531-196-3

Typesetting and origination by Pitch Publishing

Printed by TJ International Ltd, Cornwall

Contents

This book is dedicated to my brother, Mark Driver, who gave me the greatest gift one human can give to another. The gift of life.

Acknowledgements

FIRST and foremost, I'd like to thank my brother, Mark. Without him volunteering to be my kidney donor, I might not be here at all. I can never truly repay him for this huge personal sacrifice. And although this book is about me, most of what you read has only been made possible because of him.

I'd like to thank my wife, Julie, who has given me unwavering support. Despite triathlon being a very time-demanding activity, she has not once complained. In actual fact, she has been known to encourage me to get up and train when I'm tired or it's raining. (I have a sneaky suspicion this is so she can have an undisturbed lie-in, but hey, if anyone deserves it she does.)

My parents also deserve a thank-you: my dad for showing me how much fun sport can be from a young age and my mum for supporting me, despite the fact that this sport happened to be rugby. Other than base-jumping or maybe boxing, it's every mother's worst nightmare, especially when it's ingrained in them to protect their offspring, not watch them get trampled on, on cold, wet Sunday mornings throughout the winter.

I'd like to say a thank-you to all my mates who offered to donate when they heard about what was happening to me. I won't list you here – but you know who are.

Fran, my coach from Born to Train, deserves a special mention. Without his help and encouragement, my big race would have been a one-off. Instead, triathlon has now become a hobby. Every year, there's another race. And every year is a chance to go faster. (I'd also like to thank him for making me throw up on more than one occasion!)

I'd like to thank Rhys Chong at Physical Edge. Without his magic hands fixing and massaging away various aches, pains and tears, I'd be held together with string and masking tape.

All of the Greenwich Tritons, the South London Triathlon Club, have helped massively, too. Thanks for welcoming me into the fold as your typical newbie, with all the gear but no idea. And thanks for all the encouragement you gave me when I was recovering.

I couldn't thank everyone else without mentioning the company I work for, AMV, who supported me throughout. They gave unlimited time off for hospital visits, operations, sick days along with a guarantee that anything I needed, no matter what, was only a phone call away.

And last but not least, the NHS (hopefully this still exists by the time I get to the end of writing this book) and all my doctors and nurses. In particular, my surgeon Chris Callaghan, Jude in the renal clinic, Caroline in PD, Christina and Miri in donor liaison, Mani in haemodialysis and my first doctor, Dr Abbs, who encouraged me to keep going while other doctors said that what I was doing wasn't even possible.

The News

AS I read the letter, my stomach dropped. It was the results from my yearly blood test to check the function of my kidneys.

It was bad news.

Since 1996, when a routine blood test after I'd had flu showed that I had high levels of protein in my blood, I had to have an annual blood test to check my kidney function. I'd been told that high levels of protein in the blood were an early marker for kidney disease.

Every year I'd pop into hospital, get it checked and then forget about it again. In fact, the only thing that had changed in ten years was that I now had medical insurance. So instead of going to an NHS hospital, I went for my check-ups at a BUPA hospital.

This meant my doctor took notes with a fountain pen, not a Biro. There was *FHM* not *Caravanning Weekly* in the waiting room. The lady on reception offered you a complimentary cup of tea and sometimes they had Bourbon biscuits. Other than that, it was exactly the same. Same doctors, same blood tests, same results.

Thanks to the medical insurance, it technically cost me nothing. But why anyone would actually pay for better reading material, tea, biscuits and a comfier seat in the waiting room was a bit of a mystery.

I continued to read the letter. It said that my blood test results showed that my eGFR* had dropped. At this stage, I didn't really know what this meant. I just knew that it wasn't good. A high eGFR (over 60) was nothing to worry about. But a low eGFR (anything under 60) meant there could be a problem. Mine had dropped to 56.

*eGFR stands for Estimated Glomerular Filtration Rate. Put simply, it's a measure of how well your kidneys are functioning.

I would later learn how to read my blood tests and study them like a pro cycling drug tester. I'd know what was good, what was bad, what gave me hope and what gave me none. I'd even know how eating more or less of certain foods could affect it.

But at this moment in time, all I knew was that something was wrong. I carried on reading. The doctor said he suspected that a disease called IgA nephropathy was causing my kidneys damage. However, the only way to be sure was to do a biopsy. This involved numbing the area around my kidneys, sticking a large needle in my back and scraping a tiny bit off to look at under a microscope.

We had spoken about it briefly in the past. But while I felt OK and my kidney function had remained stable, I'd given it little thought.

The end of the letter said my biopsy had been booked for a week's time. I'd be seen in the morning, then I'd have to rest in bed for four to five hours afterwards before I could go home.

I stuffed the letter in my pocket and left for work. I would try not to worry about this. But the second I got into work, I did the worst thing that anyone can do if they're worried about a medical condition. I looked it up on the internet.

I read about death, kidney failure, death, transplants, death, looked up images of damaged kidneys, saw pictures of children on dialysis and found out when the first kidney transplant took place. (I also stumbled upon a clip on YouTube of a fat kid nearly falling out of his seat on a roller coaster.) But even the madness of what was on the internet couldn't disrupt my search for answers.

I signed up to an IgA nephropathy forum based in Canada. It had hundreds of other people with the same illness. Some had only just been diagnosed. Others had already had transplants. It was quite heartening to read these people's stories. It seemed like life hadn't really changed that much for most of them. But there were a few people who were on dialysis and they sounded like they were having a bit of a tough time of it. Despite this, everyone seemed immensely positive.

The thought of dialysis terrified me. I looked up pictures of it to see people plugged into giant machines. They had long pipes going into huge lumpy veins in their arms. Unsurprisingly, they all looked quite ill, too. A lot of them looked washed out and grey. To this day, I can spot a kidney patient by the colour of their skin. When I'm in reception at the hospital, I know which people will be heading up to the renal (kidney) clinic.

During this time, I read as much as I possibly could about kidneys and IgA nephropathy. The first thing I learnt is that I should have paid more attention in biology. Until now, I didn't even really know what the kidneys did.

Explained in the simplest terms possible, the kidneys filter waste products out of the blood and produce urine.

I also found out that IgA nephropathy is a type of kidney disorder that occurs when IgA-a proteins (which normally help the body fight infection) attack the kidneys. After many years, the IgA deposits may cause the kidneys to leak blood and sometimes protein into the urine. No one yet knows why this happens or why it happens to certain people. The whole disease is still a bit of mystery.

After ten to 20 years with IgA nephropathy, the kidneys can start to show signs of damage. About 25 per cent of adults with IgA nephropathy develop total kidney failure. Only five to ten per cent of children develop total kidney failure. This cheered me up a bit (not that kids get it too, but that it was an incredibly slow disease). So I'd probably be all right. But I still continued to worry about it for the next week.

I got up early and crammed myself on to the usual train. Except this time, I wasn't going to work. I was going to hospital. The Bridge Hospital at London Bridge.

I looked at everyone else enviously. They were just normal. Normal people going to work. Last week, I was just like them. Now things were going to be different. I didn't know this at the time but my life and my outlook on life would never be the same again after this visit to the hospital.

I was quite worried. I'd never been into hospital before for anything major. I'd certainly not had any treatment that involved being in a hospital bed. In fact the last time I was in one, I was wearing knitted booties and screamed if I wanted food. (Some people might say I haven't changed much.) My wife, Julie (girlfriend at the time), said she'd come with me. But I played the whole thing down and said I'd be fine, that there was nothing to worry about.

This reminded me of when I went to an entrance exam at a local private school when I was about seven years old. All the other kids were holding on to their parents' hands terrified, while I was super confident. I strolled in waving a casual goodbye to my parents before going off to fail each and every exam, quite spectacularly. Confidence in your ability can be good thing. But it helps if it's backed with at least a modicum of talent.

I hoped that the outcome of this little trip would be little more successful.

I got to reception, signed in and was given a cup of tea. As I waited, I flicked though one of the magazines. An article about the Ironman triathlon caught my eye. Recently I'd bought a bike and had started biking to work. I thought this was pretty impressive, biking a whole 12 miles to work and back everyday. But the triathlon I was reading about made my cycling to work look highly unimpressive. It started with a 2.4-mile swim, was followed by a 112-mile bike ride and finished with a marathon.

The article said the race was started by a guy called John Collins, who was a navy commander. He'd taken part in numerous triathlons in Southern California with his wife, Judy. One afternoon, him and a few friends were discussing who was the fittest out of swimmers, cyclists or runners. As a test, they decided to combine the Waikiki Rough Water Swim (2.4 miles), the Around-Oahu Bike Race (112 miles) with the Honolulu Marathon (26.2 miles). Each discipline would be completed back to back and whoever finished first would be the fittest athlete. John went on to say that the winner would be called the 'Iron Man'.

So, on 18 February 1978, 15 men set off on this incredible test of human endurance. Their support crews consisted of a few mates who'd give them water, and they had to carry their own food.

They started at 7am with minimal fanfare and only handful of spectators. Eleven hours 46 minutes and 56 seconds later Gordon Haller, a navy communications specialist from the US, was the first to be crowned Iron Man.

The guy who came second, John Dunbar, also from the US Navy, was in the lead after the second transition from bike to run. But his support crew ran out of water for him halfway through the marathon course. So they decided to give him beer instead. Needless to say, this slowed him down somewhat.

'Mr Driver. Is there a Mr Driver here?'

I was suddenly broken from my thoughts. A huge African nurse with a shiny, happy countenance was calling out my name. I stood up and followed her into a private room. She gave me a dressing gown-type thing and some weird slippers that were made out of paper.

She told me to get changed and that someone would come to collect me in a minute. In the meantime, I could watch TV and try to relax. Relax? How could I relax? I was about to have a giant needle stuck in my back, while I was still awake.

But I didn't have much time to worry. An attractive young female South African doctor came to get me and we wandered off down the corridor. Rather embarrassingly, I'd done up the gown incorrectly, so I was wandering around the hospital with my buttocks on display. The doctor pointed this out and I corrected my wardrobe malfunction.

We walked into a pristine white room that smelt strongly of disinfectant. There was a huge light above the bed and as one of the doctors adjusted it, it blinded me. Good start, I thought to myself. It was strange being in this operating room. I'd only ever seen this type of thing on TV. Probably on *Casualty* – and most of the people who ended up there died. As my mind continued down this path of reassuring thoughts, the doctor told me to get up on to the bed.

I lay down and they gave me an injection to numb the area around my kidneys. They then stuck a long thick needle into the kidney to scrape a bit off, so they could send it to the lab to study it to see what was damaging my kidneys. I could feel the blood leaking out of the hole, wetting my side. The doctor asked if I was OK. I replied 'yes, but I was very hungry and when could I eat?'

The doctor told me that in all her time doing kidney biopsies, no one had ever asked for food. I took this as a good sign. She smiled and continued with her work. It was quite an odd sensation. I could feel something moving around inside me, yet it didn't hurt at all.

It was soon over and I was back in my private room, lying down watching TV. This was better than being at home. They had a huge selection of the latest movies, a pile of magazines and the bed was surprisingly comfortable. It was more like a boutique hotel than a hospital. The nurse told me I had to lie still for three hours and not move. Easier said than done when I struggle to sit still for five minutes at the best of times.

At least I could now get something to eat. I was starving. I'd been nil by mouth since 6pm the night before. I ordered two rounds of egg and cress sandwiches, which came with an Alan Partridge-style crescent of crisps. I also noticed that there was a wine list by my bed. I'm assuming this was for visitors. Besides, I'm not sure how Julie would react to arrive and find me quaffing red wine, while lying in bed like some kind of Roman emperor in a medical gown.

I watched another film and, just as the credits rolled, Julie arrived. We left the hospital (thankfully this time I was fully dressed), signed out and got on the train. They told me they'd give me a call in eight days' time with the results.

This next week was bit of a blur. But weirdly, things pretty much went back to normal. I went back to work on the Monday as if nothing had happened. I think at times like this going back to your usual routine is probably the best thing to do, although 'normal' is rarely is used to describe the industry I work in.

At the time, I worked as a copywriter in an advertising agency called Lowe. It was a great place and it was one of the agencies I'd always wanted to work in. They had some great clients, too: Stella Artois, Reebok, Heineken, Smirnoff, Orange (the now defunct mobile company) and HSBC. I worked in the creative department with a guy called Alan, who I'd met at Leeds College. We worked in teams, one copywriter and one art director. I was the copywriter and Al was the art director.

Most creatives don't come from academic backgrounds, unlike the account handlers and planners we worked with, most of whom came from Oxford and Cambridge. Our department had mostly fallen into the job one way or another. A few had been to college or university but the others came from a wide range of different backgrounds.

The best way I can describe what a creative department is like is a cultured building site. Predominantly working-class blokes who have quite a blokey sense of humour. But they're also surprisingly cultured. You're as likely to find them in the pub or at the football as you are to see them at The Tate or in The Curzon watching a French Art House film. (I say blokes because, even in this day and age, most creatives are men. This is beginning to change for the better, with more women joining, but it's taking a very long time.)

Every few weeks, we were given a brief to work on from one of the many clients that Lowe had. Well, in theory this is how it would work. But in reality, you'd normally be working on about three things at once. Then a pitch would come in and all hell would break loose. But the department was great and there was real camaraderie, backed up by a healthy competition.

But no matter how competitive it was, we were just happy to be there. On our path from college to Lowe, we'd worked in various places up and down the country. Some OK, some bad and some terrible. But for the first time, we felt we belonged here. We'd had an unswerving focus that meant it was never 'if' but 'when' we'd get a job somewhere decent like this. It had taken a while but the day we started at Lowe was the day we knew we'd finally made it into a proper ad agency.

We'd actually had to take dramatic pay cut to be employed there. We'd gone from a big fish in small pond to a tiny fish in an ocean.

And we loved it.

Results

I SAT staring at the doctor as be gave me the news. As he spoke to me, I don't think I blinked for the entire time. He said: 'I'm sorry, but the biopsy has come back and, as I suspected, it shows IgA nephropathy.' He went on to explain that it's a type of kidney disease that could eventually completely destroy my kidneys, resulting in the need for dialysis or a transplant.

I knew this diagnosis was highly likely, as we'd spoken about it before. But now we had the results. It was a fact. For the first time in my life, I was ill. Properly ill. Not 'I'm feeling a bit under the weather, I need a bottle of Lucozade and a Yorkie' type of ill. Ill like people feel sorry for you. Ill like, when you talk about it, people want to change the subject. Ill like there'll be charities that raise money for me.

I can't remember the rest of the conversation. Everything he said just washed over me. I can only remember snippets. Blah blah blah, transplant, blah blah dialysis, blah blah, medical breakthroughs...

He finished and I sat there, motionless. He asked if I was OK and did I have any questions. I had loads but I only asked one. I wasn't aware of it at that moment but this single question would have a huge impact on me.

'Is there anything I could do to, you know, slow down the disease?'

'I'm sorry, not really. We'll give you some blood pressure drugs that will also help protect your kidneys. Apart from that, just keep fit and healthy and eat well.'

I thanked him and left. I wandered back out of the hospital and into the chaos of London Bridge Station. I wandered round for a bit not really knowing where I was going. Keep fit and healthy. I looked up at the train boards to work out when my next train was. Keep fit and healthy. My next train was only five minutes away. Keep fit and healthy. I'd be back in work in time for lunch. Keep fit and healthy…

I kept thinking about these four words. Keep. Fit. And. Healthy. If I did this, maybe my kidneys would last longer. It was worth a try. At this point, anything that might help would be worth it. It was the only thing I had to hang on to. But what should I do?

I hadn't done any proper exercise since I was 18, when I'd given up playing rugby. I could hardly start playing that again. I only weighed 13 stone. Nowadays, even amateur players were capable of playing Goliath in a movie without the need for special effects. Besides, this was supposed to help my current physical state, not finish me off completely.

I'd been to the gym for a few months at a time but never stuck to it. I found it quite dull. I can remember that I started going to a local gym after work with an old school mate called Ken (his real name is Chris but his surname is Barlow, so everyone called him Ken). We'd do our exercise, then go out for a few beers. But that turned into a few beers without the gym. The last time, we had a lot of beers, no gym and ended up going out for a kebab. There were darts players from the 70s that had a better exercise routine than this.

Last year, I'd done the London to Brighton bike ride, which was quite good fun. The part that I liked best was racing the other people. Although looking back on it now, these other riders probably had no idea that I was racing them. There were a few relatively fast riders, or so I thought at the time. But the trouble was, it wasn't a race.

You didn't get a time. And at the first hill, everyone got off and walked.

I was hardly Lance Armstrong but I wanted to race with faster people. It wasn't enough to just finish. I wanted to get a time, then try to beat it. So, I thought that's what I'd do. I'd enter again and try and beat my last time.

I had a year to go, so if started training now I'd easily beat my old time. I'd train in the same way I did last time. I'd bike to work and back every day. For a year. I'd bike in while avoiding angry cabbies, bendy buses (which are on average about 200 metres long) and just about everything else on the road that has a hatred for cyclists.

Cycling across London was akin to a mouse trying to cross a dance floor that was hosting an elephant Flamenco class. How anyone actually made it from one side to the other, on a bike, was a miracle.

On my first morning training ride to work, there were big yellow signs up warning drivers that the London Triathlon was taking place this weekend and certain roads would be closed. I thought about entering but I hadn't swum properly since I was a child. And I'd never swum in open water, except for splashing about in the Mediterranean on holiday. Plus, the pictures I'd seen in the magazine a few days earlier made the swim look like hell. Two thousand people all trying to swim over each other. It looked horrible.

I got to work, showered and changed and looked up the London Triathlon website. As I read about it, I could see there were three distances. A super sprint, a sprint and one called an Olympic. The Olympic was the longest: a 1.5km swim, a 40km bike and a 10km run. I thought about it. I could do that, couldn't I?

I'd run 10km before and London to Brighton was twice the distance of the bike ride. The one small area where would need improvement would be the swim. Well, I say improvement – I'd actually need to learn how to do it without drowning.

Before I could think of any good reasons not to enter, I found myself filling in the online form. About two minutes later, I was getting my credit card out and paying for it. I hesitated before pressing submit and then... oh shit what have I done? I was no longer doing the London Brighton. I was going for something much more challenging.

Training

I GOT in from work and eagerly told my girlfriend, Julie, that I'd entered the London Triathlon. She was a little underwhelmed.

'What have you done that for?' she asked.

I explained what the doctor had said and slowly she seemed to warm to the idea. I said I'd have to buy some kit, trainers etc, to which she rolled her eyes. She knew that I didn't need much of an excuse to spend a fortune on his type of stuff.

I'd always been a bit of nerd when it came to outdoor kit. I loved it. And I'd always buy stuff that was wholly unnecessary. For example, if I bought a fleece it would have been designed to keep mountaineers warm at -20 degrees. And I couldn't buy normal walking boots, no. I'd buy walking boots that would comfortably get you to Everest base camp and back.

Incidentally, the closest I got to anywhere like this was the Perito Moreno glacier in Argentina. And even then, there was a Japanese guy with us wearing Converse. It was hardly the death-defying ice challenge that required crampons, more's the pity. Still, I dressed like I was going to be living on the glacier for a week, not just taking pictures of it from the safety of a viewing area.

But I wasn't looking for outdoor stuff now, I was just looking for trainers. I went to Runners Need in Holborn. Firstly, they filmed how you ran so they could check your gait (your running style). Then they'd recommend some trainers. I'm sure it was purely a coincidence that they happened to be the most expensive in the shop.

They also all looked horrible. This seems to be a strange theme with running shoes. The more ridiculous your trainers look, the more you look like a serious runner. And this was before the day-glow monstrosities they sell today. Most of them look like they've been designed by Liberace on acid.

While I was in the shop, I picked up a copy of a *Triathlon* magazine. I thought this might give me a few pointers on what sort of stuff I'd need. I knew I'd have to buy a wetsuit but that was about it.

This magazine was full of stuff. And obviously it would be vitally important that I need all of it. I might not have even done a triathlon yet but that wouldn't stop me from looking like a professional. I would definitely fit into the 'all the gear, no idea' category. The other thing I had to do was actually start training.

So, with my new trainers, an old T-shirt and a baggy pair of knee-length combat shorts, I set off on my first run. I'd decided to run from where I lived in Bromley to Blackheath and back. This seemed easy enough but after about 20 minutes I felt knackered. I was a lot less fit than I thought.

I slowly walked back home realising that I'd probably bitten off more than I could chew. I looked through the mag I'd bought and I had an idea. There must be training programmes on the internet. I'd look for one on there for a novice and then at least I'd have some structure.

I found a programme that suited my needs but it only had a 20-week plan. I had about 50 until the race.

In my limited knowledge, I thought I could start it now then just keep doing it for the next 30 weeks until the race. I can see now that this was ridiculous. But back then, I really had no idea what I was doing.

I kept up the running and slowly but surely I started to improve. It wasn't long before I could run for about an hour without having to worry that I needed to follow a route where there were plenty of bus stops, so I could get a lift home.

I also managed to get over a condition known as the 'runner's trots'. Every time I went for a run about 30 minutes in, I needed to go to the toilet. That's fine if you're running around a park with toilets but not so good if said toilets are out of order.

I can remember a time I was running into work in the morning. About half way there, I felt like I needed to go, so I slowly jogged to the usual toilets. But, on this occasion, they were closed. Fine, I thought, I'll just wait until I get to work. However, the situation became a bit more desperate as I carried on running. This was to be my first proper race against time.

I quickened my pace. Oh no, this could be really embarrassing. By the time I was about one kilometre from work, I was running flat out, red-faced and, well, I've no idea what my running looked like but it certainly wouldn't be held up as good form. With buttocks clenched and a pained expression, I started to look around for somewhere to go where a) I wouldn't be seen; and b) not get arrested. But I couldn't see anywhere.

The agency I worked in was in Knightsbridge, a very posh part of London. There are a lot of beautiful, very big, expensive houses in this area. And they all have large gardens, which at this present moment in time looked very inviting. I'm not sure how the Duchess of Mingford would react to wake up and see me, shorts round my ankles, defecating in her garden. But I'm pretty sure it wouldn't end with an invite to her annual garden party.

It was looking like this was going to be the only option. Just then, out of the corner of my eye, I spotted a builder's portaloo. I'd been in these before at Glastonbury and it was never a pleasant experience. But this was now my only option. I swung the door open and, in one move, dropped my shorts and sat down.

It was spotless. There was a stack of soft, white, pristine loo paper and the lock on the door worked. The only thing missing was cherubic angles to serenade me as I loudly emptied my bowels. I'd made it in the nick of time. Even the water pump worked on the sink. I washed my hands and left. Thankfully, this was the last time this happened. Well, the last time it happened on the way to work anyway.

Apart from this minor mishap, my training was actually beginning to make some progress. My running was improving. I was cycling into work and back about three days a week. But I really needed to start swimming. I also needed to buy a wetsuit.

I did little or no research to find a wetsuit. I searched the internet for a triathlon shop that was close to work and jumped on a tube. Unbelievably, there weren't many places that sold tri stuff back then, so I had to go all the way to Wimbledon.

I went in and proudly told the assistant in a loud voice, so the rest of the shop could hear, that I had entered the London Triathlon, yes *The London Triathlon*, and I needed a wetsuit. The other guy and girl in the shop ignored me completely. But deep down, I thought they were probably pretty impressed.

The guy there was incredibly helpful and not patronising at all, unlike some of the assistants you get in high-end bike shops. Most of the time, if you haven't hand-built your bike yourself, regularly rode around the Alps and had legs smoother than a supermodel's, they can barely be bothered to give you a second look, never mind help you.

I told him that this was my first race, so he recommended one for me to try on. I picked the size that looked about right and he asked if I knew how to put it on. I lied and said yes.

I tried it on in the changing room. To anyone who was in the shop at the time, it must have looked like I was wrestling a bear in there. No matter how much I wriggled and strained, I couldn't get it on for love nor money. (Something else I discovered was how hot you get trying on a wetsuit indoors. I was dripping.)

So, when I finally appeared from behind the curtain, covered in sweat and barely able to breath, looking like a vacuum-packed cretin, it was a relief to be told that I'd picked up the wrong size. I needed a couple of sizes up.

Just as he told me this, the couple I was trying to impress left the shop and the guy wished them good luck at The European Championships at the weekend. They must have thought I was a right wally.

One good thing about my choice to do the London Triathlon is that it's great for beginners. They sent me a pack with all the info. Plus, they had a swim training course where we could have a guided swimming lesson in the dock that we'd be swimming in for the actual race.

By now I'd roped in one of my mates, a guy called Rog I'd known since school, to race with me. So I sent him the e-mail and we signed up to do the swim training together. In two weeks' time, I would try my first open water swim. This was quite exciting – and a little bit scary.

It's the swim that really scares first-time triathletes the most. Cycling and running is the easy bit. I would eventually find out that this definitely wasn't the case but at this moment in time the swim was the only part of the race I was worrying about. I guess it's fear of the unknown. It was nowhere near as scary as what was happening to my kidneys but it did worry me a bit. Obviously, I didn't tell anyone else this.

The time of the swim training started at 8am. They recommended a light meal no later than two hours before the swim. A brief calculation meant I'd have to get up and eat at 5.30am. Who's awake at this time? Milkmen maybe. New-born babies?

It wasn't so long ago I'd be coming home from a club at this time. But things had changed. I had just signed up, voluntarily, to get up in the middle of the night and then go swimming in a London dock.

My mates told me I was having a mid-life crisis. Maybe this was true but poncing around in a wetsuit was better than buying a Harley and running off with a girl half my age.

I'd find out later that getting up stupidly early is actually relatively easy. It takes the body on average 30 days to get used to a new routine. Once it's established, it becomes automatic. At the moment, though, getting up at this time and forcing myself to eat breakfast was anything but automatic.

Having said that, getting up in the cold and dark to eat and then go swimming made me feel like a professional athlete. The only thing I was lacking was the incredible natural talent they possess – and the commitment. So while I felt like the real deal, I was actually nothing like a proper athlete.

I arrived at the venue and met my mate Rog, who looked even more nervous than I did. This made me feel a bit better. The first thing that struck me was how dirty the water looked and how cold it was. But once in the water, you warmed up surprisingly quickly. My wetsuit was certainly doing its job. It also made me much more buoyant so drowning would be much harder. This little thought cheered me up.

We did a few drills then took it in turns to swim out to a buoy about 200m away. As I swam out, I could see nothing. Swimming through tar would have been clearer. I couldn't even see the end of my hand as I swam. Plus, I noticed that while I thought I was swimming in a straight line I was actually swimming quite far to the left. If I continued, I'd either swim in a complete circle or end up swimming out of the dock, down the Thames and out to sea.

The guy who was running the course explained that sighting was incredibly important. You should pick something on the other side of the bank. A flagpole, a tree, anything that you could see from the water and swim towards it. As we were near City Airport, I picked a windsock. This made a huge difference. I could now swim in a straight line. I was knackered after just 200m out and 200m back. But I could work on that.

I'd now covered everything. I could swim in a straight line, I could ride my bike without falling off and I could run without having to make emergency stops. All I needed to do now was some brick training which, according to my programme, meant a bike session followed by a run, and I'd be ready. What's more, I still had 20 weeks to go. This would be easy.

During this time, I had another blood test and my doctor, a guy called Ian Abbs, told me that my eGFR had dropped slightly to 54. He said it was not a major drop and I shouldn't be too worried. I told him that I'd entered the London Triathlon and he seemed suitably impressed. He just told me to be careful that I didn't drown in the swim. Apparently, someone had drowned the year before. Well, thanks for that.

I now had just ten weeks to go. All I had to do was keep up my maximum week's training every week from now until the race. This was a mistake. I had no idea about peaking for a race. I was still of the school of thought that's faster, longer, harder.

With eight weeks to go, I had a tight stabbing pain in my knee after 40 minutes of running. Like all sensible amateur triathletes, I ignored this hoping it would go away. Of course, it didn't. It just got worse and worse until I couldn't run for more than five minutes without the pain being excruciating. There wasn't much else to do other than go to the doctor's then to the physio.

The physio I saw was a guy called Rhys from a place called Physical Edge. He told me I had ITB Syndrome, a common condition caused by tight muscles. The band that runs down the outside of your thigh becomes tighter and rubs against the knee. He asked me what stretches I did. Erm... stretches? I didn't do any.

It was a swift learning curve. After every session, I should stretch. I told him how long I'd been training without stretching and he was surprised it hadn't happened earlier. I now had to manually stretch my ITB by rolling around on a foam roller. I looked like a human seesaw, rolling backwards and forwards. Every other day, I'd go and see Rhys for 30 minutes of torture. He'd lean on my leg with his forearm and push up and down on it to stretch my ITB. It was agony.

While he was doing it, he'd talk to me (mainly to try and help take my mind off the pain) about some of the other people he treated. He'd tell me about his friend, a coach who was training for his fifth Ironman. This event still fascinated me, but it was still something I would never consider myself.

After a couple of weeks of this torture, it started to get better. I could run again, I was swimming weekly at the Tooting Bec Lido in my wetsuit. and my cycling was good, too. I'd even done few brick sessions.

I'd bike home, run upstairs, put on my trainers and do half an hour's run. I'd still be wearing my bike shorts and top but this is what I planned to race in. Occasionally, the local kids would shout 'Oi, bender!' at me as I ran passed. But other than that, it was coming on nicely.

According to my training plan, it was now time to taper. Nowadays when I taper, I up the intensity but lower the distance. This time, I just took it easy and did all my training slowly. Slow runs, slow bike rides and slow swims. To be honest, I didn't really do any of these particularly quickly, so my training actually changed very little.

I was now ready… well, as ready as I'd ever be, to do my first race.

The London Triathlon Part 1

THE night before, I laid out all my equipment and checked it. Then I packed it all away then, to be on the safe side, unpacked it all and checked it again. I was close to doing it a third time. I was so paranoid about leaving something behind. That's the thing with triathlon, there's so much stuff. Great for gadget geeks but not so good for forgetful people who are borderline OCD.

My race time was 8am. So I'd have to eat at 6am at the latest, which meant setting the alarm for 5am. I had a large plate of pasta prepared for me by Julie to carb-load and then I went to bed at about 10pm to get an early night.

11pm, still awake. Shit, I'm not tired at all. 12am, still not tired. 1am, bollocks, I've got to get up in four hours... I must have finally dozed off soon after. A few hours later, my alarm woke me up. I'd been fast asleep. It was one of those really deep sleeps where you forget what day it is and what you're supposed to be doing. Then I remembered, it was race day.

I went downstairs quietly, so Julie could have a bit more of a lie-in while I made breakfast. I'd have banana and peanut butter bagels and start sipping energy drink. I sat in the living room, checking one last time that I had everything. Then the smoke alarm went off.

I'd bought a Dualite toaster a few years earlier because I thought it looked cool. And it did. But it was a terrible toaster. Anything bigger than wafer-thin slices bread got stuck in it, then burned, then set off the smoke alarm. It regularly burned bagels, crumpets and muffins to a crisp. Most of the time, it would have been quicker for me to just set my bread on fire.

I slowly ate my burnt bagels, occasionally spitting out bits of soot. I didn't need any coffee as my adrenaline had already made sure I was wide awake by now. I loaded all my stuff into the car and we headed off towards to London's Excel Centre in the pitch dark.

There were hundreds of cars queuing to get in. Some of the bikes didn't even look like bikes. They were shiny carbon dream machines with wheels that were just discs. They didn't even have any spokes. They looked like bikes from another planet. My bike was carbon but it didn't even have road bike handlebars.

I unloaded the car and headed off to transition, the place where you put your bike and running stuff and dump your wetsuit (if you make it out of the swim alive).

A couple of the other guys chatted to me. Some were doing it for the first time, like me. Others had been doing it for years. Some had old aluminium bikes. Others had bikes that were worth more than my car. Reassuringly, not everyone was an expert.

I put on my wetsuit and immediately needed the toilet. It was quite strange to be wandering around in public looking like an overweight catwoman after a sex change. But at least I was surrounded by like-minded people.

As I walked to the toilet, I noticed the T-shirt wars of triathlon. No one talks about it but those who have raced will know what I mean.

There's the newbies like me who are proudly wearing a 10km finishers T-shirt. I fitted into the class of 'just runners'. Then there are the old hands at Olympic distance, who wear their T-shirts. Then there's the middle-distance T-shirts and, in my eyes at the time, the king of the T-shirts – the Ironman finishers T-shirt. This seemed like such an unachievable goal. I was pretty impressed by anyone who'd done it.

(There's also the age group GB T-shirts; the Norseman T-shirts, a brutal Iron distance race that starts by jumping off a tanker into a freezing fjord and finishes with a marathon up a mountain; and Enduroman T-shirts, a race that is for the clinically insane. It's multiples of the Iron distance, the longest being ten Ironmans, back to back to back. There were many others but at this time I only heard of a few races.)

Anyway, I finally got to the toilet to discover that everyone who was racing also needed to go. I queued for what seemed like ages before running back to my transition. The guy next to me was covering his feet and arms with baby oil. I asked what he was doing and he told me that it would help him get out of his wetsuit easier. He lent me some and I did the same. I'm happy to say this was first time I'd chatted to a guy dressed in a rubber suit while handing round a bottle of baby oil.

The announcer called all the 8am racers to the start to go through the safety chat. I was too nervous and excited to listen to too much of this. The only bit I remember was the bit about lying on your back and raising your arm in the air if you got into trouble during the swim. A guy in a canoe would then come over to you and rescue you.

There was just enough time to kiss Julie goodbye, hopefully not for the last time, before I walked down to the steps to the water's front. I had nothing to fear, except fear itself. Well, that and drowning.

OK, here goes. Breathe, relax, take deep breaths and focus. I got into the water and swam a bit to warm up. In my excitement, I'd forgotten my plan to start at the back and I settled myself right at the front.

The announcer counted down from five, then a loud horn went off and I was away. It was total chaos. There were arms, feet, heads and splashing water everywhere. I got my goggles kicked off, took a massive gulp of water and choked. I was kicked in the face and someone accidently elbowed me in the back of the head. It was very much a case of swim blindly forwards and hope for the best. Any sighting or strategy went right out the window.

However, after about five minutes, I managed to find some clear water. I slowed down a bit, focused on the big yellow buoy 750m away and started to get into my rhythm. Apart from the first few minutes, this wasn't bad at all. I don't know what I'd been so worried about.

After what seemed like an eternity, I was at the yellow buoy. I was halfway through. I had a little celebratory wee in my wetsuit before looking at my watch. It had taken me about 16 minutes. Not bad. I'd thought it would take about 35 minutes, so I was ahead of my expected time.

My arms were getting really tired now. My legs were fine because I didn't really kick at all. Again, a big mistake, but in my wisdom I was saving them for the bike and run. I've since learnt that is nonsense. Not kicking causes your legs to drop and actually makes it harder for your arms to drag you through the water, using up valuable energy.

I kept ploughing on and I could now hear the crowd and see the jetty. Just a little bit further and I'd be out. I crawled out of the water with all the style and elegance of a mudskipper making its first foray on to land. Someone helped me out of the water and, even though I was incredibly light-headed, I was alive. I'd done it. I staggered around like a drunken toddler, trying to get my balance. Eventually, I steadied myself and took off my wetsuit, put it into the bag I was given and jogged off towards transition. I suddenly realised I'd forgotten where my bike was.

I searched up and down and luckily I was one of the only people on a hybrid bike, so it didn't take me long. I put on my trainers and headed off on to the course. On the bike course, I felt surprisingly good. I even started to overtake a few people with much better bikes than me. I was loving this. For the first time since I was kid playing rugby, I was competing. I'd forgotten how competitive I was.

I never really showed it overtly but I loved the challenge of competition. The bike course was flat and fast, and was easily my favourite part. I looked down at my bike bottle and suddenly remembered that I had to eat and drink. I had a bottle of Lucozade sport and a couple of energy gels. I drank the drink, dropped one of the gels and managed to swallow the second. This wasn't the 'little and often' style of eating and drinking that I'd read about. But it would do.

I went round the loop at the end of Embankment, the road next to the Thames, and before I knew it I'd finished the first loop. I was halfway through. Time-wise, I was still well on target to beat the three hours I'd set myself.

The rest of the bike flew by. I was soon back in the huge Excel Centre. I could see and hear other people finishing. Others were just arriving with all their stuff while I was right in the middle of my race. I felt good and strong. I racked my bike and ...Jesus, what's happened to my legs? They felt like jelly. I was knackered.

I was about to find out that the real race in triathlon starts with the run or, in my case, the shuffle. I only had 10km to run but at this moment in time that felt like a hell of a long way. About 3km in, my legs started to feel a bit better. But I couldn't speed up. I had nothing. I just had to keep running. Don't stop. Whatever you do, don't stop.

I ran past a couple of guys who were walking. This gave me a bit of a boost. But considering they were walking, I hardly sped past them. At the end of the second loop, I saw Julie. She screamed encouragement at me and again this energised me. I started to speed up a little. I waved and smiled.

In my mind, I had a mantra of 'don't stop, don't stop, don't stop'. One of the support crews that are dotted around the course handed me a cup of energy drink. I spilled most of it down my front and got it in my eyes. A couple of sips made it into my mouth, though.

I also took an energy gel. I bit into it and it squirted all over my face, giving me a sickly sweet money shot. I must have looked like I was melting. I was just hoping to finish soon before I started to attract a swarm of wasps to my gel-covered, sugar-coated face.

I could now see the finish. I started to speed up. My lungs were burning but I was going to finish. I started to lose the feeling in my legs. Faster, faster. I was now flat out. My vision was beginning to go. Faster, faster. I overtook a few more people as I went flying down the finishing tunnel and over the line. Covered in snot, sweat, energy gels and Lucozade, I bent down to catch my breath. Dizzy with exhaustion. I'd never felt anything like it. For a brief moment, it gave me an idea of what it meant when athletes say they gave it everything.

One of the support crews put a medal around my neck and I staggered off to find Julie. I'd successfully finished my first race. It was two hours 43 minutes, 17 minutes faster than my predicted time – and I'd loved every second of it. As I found out later, I'd also beaten Rog. His pre-race meal had been a fried egg and bacon bagel, which he ate when we arrived. He was then sick during the swim and felt rough for the rest of the race.

For the remainder of the day, I felt great. Tired but great. I didn't think about my kidneys once. I was a triathlete. I'd done something that only about one per cent or less of the population gets to achieve. I wasn't ill. I was fitter than most of the people in the country. And knowing this made me feel good.

Besides, 'triathlete' sounded better than 'kidney disease patient.' I wasn't aware of this at the time but triathlon would help me massively when it came to coping with my illness, both mentally and physically.

As long I kept this up, I felt I could deal with it. If I was going to have this illness, I was going to be the fittest kidney disease patient in the world, well Europe. OK, the UK. Whatever, I felt like I was ready for it to do its worst.

Dealing With It

AFTER another visit to the hospital, I was told that my kidneys had got a little worse. The doctor this time started to explain a bit more about my blood tests and what they'd be looking for.

Now I was established as a kidney patient and had a diagnosis of IgA nephropathy, they would mainly be checking the levels of my creatinine in my blood. It's a waste product that's excreted by the muscles and removed from the blood by the kidneys. The higher the level, the worse it showed my kidney function was. My creatinine was currently at 125. This meant that I had Stage 2 kidney disease.

From now on, I would check my creatinine after every blood test. My doctor told me that it was all about the overall trend. He expected it to slowly go up. But he also warned me that IgA nephropathy was a very variable disease. In some cases, it could go on for years and I'd die of old age before my kidneys failed. But in others, it could suddenly speed up and cause them to fail within two years. It was like having the sword of Damocles hanging over me.

I asked again if there was anything I could do to keep my kidneys healthy. The doctor just told me to keep doing what I was doing. He also said that my training regime was certainly helping to keep my blood pressure low. High blood pressure is very dangerous to the kidneys. It's known as the silent killer.

Outwardly, high blood pressure has no symptoms. It can damage the kidneys for years and you'll only discover it when it's too late. So if you've never had your blood pressure checked, do so. Who knows, it could save your life. Well, your kidneys anyway.

Having been officially diagnosed, I started to look at life slightly differently. It's a cliché but life is a gift – and you only realise how much so when something happens.

People say 'it puts things into perspective' when something terrible happens. But you should live your life from that perspective all the time. Because, take it from me, you never know what's around the corner. As I contemplated this, I made a decision. I'd ask Julie to marry me.

We'd already been together for around 12 years and, while we'd talked about it, we'd always delayed it to spend one more Christmas travelling. We'd take the last week off before Christmas, all of the Christmas holidays and another week the other side. This normally gave us around 24 days off.

We'd been lucky enough to visit some amazing places and do some incredible things.

We'd been motor-biking in the Vietnamese highlands. Julie fell off her bike and damaged her knee. This didn't stop her, however. She just drank more of the local rice wine and got on with it. (I hasten to add that she wasn't driving, she was on a guide's bike).

We'd travelled around Burma while being followed around by their secret police, a dodgy-looking guy in a black leather jacket with Aviators, who mysteriously appeared wherever we were – no matter where we were staying in the country.

We'd done the Inca trail in Peru, led by the cheesiest man I've ever met, a Peruvian guy in a chino suit with slicked back hair, who said 'Heeey Chicos' a lot, while giving a double thumbs-up. He was like a South American Fonzy.

We'd even been lucky enough to visit India, a country where people think it's normal to send motorbikes through the post. You share train carriages with live monkeys and cows are allowed to wander around supermarkets.

But this year, it was time I made an honest woman of her. God forbid, if something dramatic happened, I want her and everyone else to know how much I loved her.

I decided that I'd book a surprise trip to New York at Christmas and I'd ask her there. I also decided to enter the London Triathlon again and another Olympic distance race in Windsor.

I'd acquired most of the kit I needed now but the one thing I really wanted was a new bike. I now experience this want on a weekly basis and if I had infinite funds I'd probably have hundreds. But unfortunately, I don't. So I'd have to settle for one.

I didn't really know much about bikes then. I knew that carbon was light but that was about it. There was one thing I was certain of, though. I wanted it to look good.

I headed off to Evans Cycles by London Bridge and it was here I bought my first proper road bike. A shiny black carbon Bianchi C2C. It looked awesome. To me at this point, that's all that really mattered.

To my shock, it didn't come with any pedals. £1,000 and no pedals? It's like buying a car and the finding out you have to pay extra for the wheels.

The guy in the shop showed me various pedals. But he said what I really needed were clipless pedals, which, weirdly, are the pedals you clip your feet into. I chose some that cost around £80. And, of course, if I bought these, I'd have to buy some bike shoes, too. Another £65.

Oh, and I'd need bottle cages. Bottles. A small bag to carry the inner tubes. Inner tubes and, while you're at it, I'll have a new top with some socks to match.

I finally left the shop about £1,500 worse off. But I didn't really care because I had a new bike. A proper bike. A carbon road bike. There was just one slight problem. I'd never ridden a bike with my feet clipped in, so I'd have to take it home on the train. Central London didn't seem like the safest place to test them out. And I'm glad I waited until I got home, otherwise I might not be here now.

Julie said I loved the bike more than her, which obviously isn't true. But I did keep it in the dining room for the first six months and I spent an unhealthy amount of time admiring it.

The other slightly more pressing thing I had to do was learn to ride it with clipless pedals. So I cycled off slowly down the road where I lived. While I was moving, I was fine. Stopping, on the other hand, proved a lot more tricky. I got to a small junction, wobbled, failed to unclip and fell off in front of a load of kids, who cracked up.

I'd cut my elbow but it was pride that bore the brunt of this accident. Unperturbed by this minor accident, I spent the rest of the afternoon biking round the quiet back roads where I lived, stopping occasionally to unclip, or fall off. I'd become the cycling equivalent of a weeble. But after a while, I got the hang of it.

Greenwich
Tritons

I T was round about now that I decided to join a triathlon
club, too. Not only would I be able to train with other
people, I'd also be able to pick the brains of other more
experienced athletes. My closest club was a tri club in Greenwich called The Greenwich Tritons. Every Saturday, they'd
meet up on Blackheath to ride into Kent. There was a novice
ride, a group two (for intermediates) and a group one ride. This
was the fittest and fastest group. I signed up on the website and
agreed to meet them on a sunny Saturday morning.

There was quite a mixed bunch. There were novices like
me, people who'd been doing it for a few years, the more
experienced athletes who'd been doing it for most of their
lives and some who had represented their country at various
distances. One of them had even competed at the Olympics
(although to this day I've never actually met her.)

I'd spent the last month doing nothing but cycling. It was
like I was training to go training with these guys. I turned up
at the meeting point, introduced myself and they suggested
I ride with group two. Up until now, I'd only ever commuted.
I'd never been out into the Kent countryside. The views were
certainly more impressive than the ones I saw riding though
Bermondsey.

The other thing I noticed was how hilly it was. There are no hills whatsoever in London. There are a few minor inclines but nothing compared to what I was riding now. This was proper cycling and I was knackered. I didn't realise this at the time but this was just a training ride. But to me, every hill became a race. So I pushed harder and faster than ever before. The next week, I'd ride with group one. I was ready... wasn't I?

In preparation for the group one ride on Saturday, I didn't go out for a beer on Friday with work, which is easier said than done when you work in advertising. If you don't drink, people assume there's something wrong with you. So I had a coke, had the mickey taken out of me for 20 minutes and headed off home.

The next morning my alarm didn't go off, so I woke up late. I didn't have time for breakfast, so I just skipped it and headed off to Blackheath, where the Tritons met. We started the ride all together but the novice group soon dropped back and the group two left us and went in another direction. It was just me and four other guys left.

One of them had done an Ironman the week before, so we'd be taking it fairly easy, right? Wrong. The first hour or so was OK but they were riding much faster than I'd ever been. And the fact I hadn't eaten anything made this one of the hardest rides I'd ever done.

I held on by the skin of my eyelids for the next three hours. A couple of them gave me some of their food, which just about kept me alive. But to be honest, the only thing that would have enabled me to keep up with them was hard drugs. I was knackered. I'd never been so tired. My legs felt like lead weights, my lungs were bursting and everyone muscle and piece of sinew in my body was screaming to stop. But I carried on.

I'd like to say it was incredible stamina that got me through this ride but it was sheer bloody-mindedness and the fear of looking like a total fool. It was also the fact that they slowed down to wait for me.

(Since finishing this book, one of the guys who was leading this ride has gone on to win the double Ironman World Championship. Obviously he wasn't riding anywhere near flat out but it gives you an idea of the level of a group one ride).

Finally, we made it back to towards Blackheath, I thanked them for nearly killing me and slowly biked off home. I staggered in and collapsed on the sofa. I was so tired I could barely move. Julie nursed me back to life with pasta and sugary tea.

Up until this point, I still thought I was quite fit. And, I guess, compared to most people I was. But some of these guys (and girls) were seriously fit.

So from now on, I'd ride with group two most Saturdays. They also had running on a Wednesday and swimming on a Thursday and Sunday. I trained through the year and slowly got fitter. By the time The Windsor Triathlon had come round, I felt much fitter than I had the year before. I'd also managed to get a friend of mine into it, a guy called Mark Folbigg.

I'd been mates with him at school since we were 13 and we'd played rugby together. I'm not sure why I persuaded him to join me in this race because he's one of those people who's naturally gifted at sport. You name it, darts, running, skiing. Whatever sport he turned his hand to, he was good at it – and now he was going to be racing with me. I was ready to be beaten, again. It was all good natured but I still really wanted to beat him. Maybe this time would be different.

A week before the race, I'd had another trip to the doctor's. As suspected, my kidney function had lowered again. My creatinine was now 140. Still nothing to worry about and there was nothing I could do anyway. My blood pressure was excellent. So I could just keep on doing what I was doing.

Besides, I was only a week away from my second Olympic distance triathlon and I felt great, so it didn't really worry me. The doctor talked briefly about what could happen in the future and that I'd be a good candidate for a pre-emptive transplant from a family member. This is where they give you a transplant before your kidneys fail, so you can avoid dialysis. It sounded good to me. But then it would. I had no idea how my family would react, though…

'What would you like for Christmas this year?'

'Erm… a kidney?'

What? I was thinking more along the lines of a voucher from Wiggle.'

But I didn't need to worry about this yet. I'd recently read that people only start dialysis when their creatinine reaches around 800. A quick calculation revealed that my kidneys would probably be OK until I was about 70. I'd take that. It's funny how you start making bargains with yourself when you're ill, especially as you have no control of what will happen when.

Windsor

INSTEAD of just sticking my bike in the back of the car, I decided to buy a bike carrier from Halfords. I found one in the store that looked relatively easy to assemble. But I wanted to be sure. I tried to get some help from one of the assistants, a young guy who looked like he'd had about an hour's sleep. I asked if the model I was looking at could carry more than one bike. He just stared at me, blinking. He sighed and mustered a 'dunno' before walking off. I say walked, it was more of a shuffle, like a zombie from George A. Romero horror film.

Back at home, I emptied the contents of the box all over the driveway. It seemed like everything was there. Well, everything but the instructions.

I spent the next hour building a contraption so ornate and weird looking that it could have been shortlisted as a sculpture for the Turner Prize. I had now assembled and dismantled it about six times. I couldn't for the life of me work out how this contraption fitted together.

After about an hour, I'd totally lost patience and kicked the box across the driveway. (This anger at inanimate objects, when trying to fix them/put them together, is one of the many traits I've inherited from my dad.) However, on this occasion, it helped. It caused the missing instructions to fly out.

After reading these, it was actually quite simple. It didn't seem very stable but the ropes that tucked into the boot would make it impossible for it fall off. So even if the worst did happen, my new bike would just be dragged down the road while being connected to the car by small pieces of rope. It wouldn't bounce off and crash into the windscreen of a following car, causing a multiple pile-up, which was nice to know.

I then set about packing and repacking my bag, making sure I had all my kit, and remembering to take the hotel confirmation. I was ready to go and meet my old friend, Mark, and his girlfriend, (now wife) Zoe.

We arrived at Lenny Henry's favourite hotel, a Premier Inn, to see Mark fiddling with his bike. He had a decent aluminium road bike that a friend had built for him. I'd brought my new bike and my hybrid too in case he wanted to borrow it. He couldn't decide which to use. Mark was a fast runner but when it came to making a decision, he could make a sloth seem impulsive. I reminded him that the race started in 18 hours and left him to it.

We checked into the hotel and asked for an alarm call. Our wave started at 7.20am. This meant getting up at 5am to eat. The girls weren't too happy about this, so we agreed to meet in the corridor to have breakfast. Mark had brought a toaster with him, so we could plug it in outside the room while we let the girls have (a bit) more of a lie-in.

After popping into Windsor to get something to eat, we stopped at a pub for a pint (of lime and soda), which took less than 60 seconds to drink. Pubs when you're not drinking really are a total waste of time. Then we went to bed to try to get some sleep. Fat chance.

This time it wasn't nerves that were keeping me awake. It was the couple next door having loud, rampant sex. (Not Mark and Zoe, I hasten to add.) It was coming from the room the other side of ours. Oh well, I thought, it'll be over in a minute. Two hours later, they were still banging like a barn door in a gale. She was squealing so loudly it sounded like someone was in there brutally killing livestock. However, I managed to doze off eventually.

The alarm went off and I crept outside in my boxers to meet Mark. We plugged in the toaster and toasted the bagels. Added the banana and peanut butter and tried to chew and swallow this crusty, dry but energising breakfast. It's very difficult to wake yourself up in the middle of the night and start eating. But from past experience of skipping breakfast, this was better than the alternative.

As we stood there in our pants eating, Ron Jeremy and Porky started again... give the poor girl a break or she won't be able to walk tomorrow. I'm guessing she wasn't racing. If she was, her running style would have been interesting. I went off back to bed for an hour before it was time to get up and go to the start.

The phone rang and it scared the hell out of me. I was already awake but it made me jump out of my skin. I mumbled 'thanks' to the receptionist, or whoever it is that gets lumbered with making these calls. I drew back the curtains and looked out of the window to see the sun rising. It looked like it was going to be a beautiful, clear summer's day and, more importantly, a calm one. Because the swim was in the Thames – 750m against the flow of the river and 750m with it. If I could survive the first half, the second bit would be easy.

As we left the room, we saw the couple from next door. I'm not sure what I expected them to look like but in my mind I imagined them to be younger and certainly better looking. They must have been doing it with the light off. He had a face that looked like a ball bag on a cold day, like a tiny, purple, pickled fig. And she had a face like an omelette.

We drove to the start, laid all our stuff out and went to join the rest of our wave. It was surprisingly small. I think there were only about 40 of us, so it would be a lot easier to find some space to swim than it had been at London.

The announcer told us to get into the water and get ready for the start. Three, two, one and we were off. I was swimming but I didn't seem to be making much ground. Because of the current, I swam sharply off to the left and into a boat. As I tried to swim back to the middle of the river, I could feel the bottom of the riverbed.

I actually stopped and stood up at one point. It was only waist deep. I corrected my angle and carried on swimming straight into the sun. I had no idea where I was going, so I was relieved to eventually see the turnaround buoy ahead.

I turned and swum with the current back to the start. This was better. I felt like a dolphin cutting through the water. I could have swam faster than my usual pace if I'd just floated down the river, just like all the other turds that are no doubt bobbing around in the Thames.

I got to the finish and, as I was pulled out of the water, I could see Mark ahead of me. It was his first race and he was ahead of me already. But I knew I'd make up time on the bike and then it would just be a case of hoping he didn't catch me on the run – although I knew this was highly likely.

As predicted, I caught Mark on the bike, overtook him and then tried to get as far in front of him as I possibly could.

Apart from this the bike was fairly uneventful, relatively flat with a great run-in back to Windsor. You could easily hit 70kph. We entered back into the main part of Windsor and there was a surprisingly big crowd. After London, I knew the run would be the hard bit. Windsor would be even harder because we had to run up the hill in the centre of town four times. It was going to hurt, especially for someone whose running is their weak point.

This is where the pain started. Again and again and again. My quads were burning. The sun had come out now too, making it incredibly hot – and it was only about 10am. I didn't envy the people stating at midday. After the first lap, I saw Mark just starting his run. So unless I completely fell apart, it was unlikely that he'd catch me.

I kept it together and with one kilometre to go I went flat out, pushing as hard as I dared. With about 200m to go, my legs started to go bit wobbly, so I staggered over the finishing line. Slower than London but this had been a much harder course. I'd done it again. Me 1, kidney disease 0. And I'd also beaten Mark.

Julie and Zoe both greeted us and congratulated us. It had been a great race, with decent support from all the locals, and there were plenty of nice pubs, so we could have a well-earned pint and a full Sunday roast. In fact, the only thing that was a bit disappointing was the fact that you didn't get a medal. You just got a T-shirt. Still, it meant I could now compete in the T-shirt wars when I raced in London again in a few months' time.

I continued training with the club and got to know quite a few people there. There was a group who I'd ride with most Saturdays. It made the longer rides much more enjoyable. Plus, it helped me learn a lot of new rides around Kent.

I'm quite lucky in that where I live we can be out into the countryside in about 30 minutes and into the North Downs in about 45 minutes.

But in between these times, I continued to use two commutes a week as part of my training.

A week after Windsor, I started training again. It was a bright sunny Monday morning and I got on my bike and rode off on my usual route to work. I'd go from Grove Park, then across to Blackheath, a large open space in south-east London where thousands of people were apparently buried after the Black Death.

When I first moved to this area of London I looked up this story but found there is actually no evidence of this at all. A less grisly but more plausible suggestion for the origin of the name, which was recorded as early as the 11th century, is that it stems from Old English words meaning 'dark soil'. But still, the Black Death version makes for a more interesting story.

I'd then ride through Greenwich Park. So far, so nice and pleasant. From here, it would go down hill. I'd head towards Deptford. Famous for... erm. Well, the only thing I'd ever seen happen here of any note was kids firing fireworks at me as I biked through it one evening on 5 November. I'd then go through Surrey Quays and into Bermondsey.

This has changed dramatically in the last ten years. It used to be rough and neglected. Now the developers have taken over. Borough market has transformed the area and a one-bedroom flat now goes for around £450,000.

From here, it would be great. Over Tower Bridge, down the Embankment next to the Thames, all the way to Big Ben. Then it was only another ten minutes until I arrived at work. All in all, it would take me about an hour to ride 22km. With the return journey, I'd have another two hours riding in the tank.

But that was how it usually worked out. Today, a woman driving a Golf GTi had other ideas. As I overtook a jam of cars queuing down the road in Deptford checking for idicat... smash! Suddenly, I was flying over the bonnet of her car.

I must have landed on my hand because my glove was torn and it was bleeding. As I sat up and looked around, the first thing I saw was a woman who screamed at me. She was shaking and crying.

I stood up, not sure what was going on and tried to calm her down. But she then started hyperventilating. She was having a panic attack. I'd completely forgotten about what had just happened as I tried to calm her down. I sat her down by the side of the road and slowly she returned to normal. It was only at this point that I realised she was the driver of the car. She'd just run me over and I was sitting beside her trying to comfort her, telling her everything would be all right.

She'd got tired of being stuck in the traffic jam and decided to take another route. This is when she pulled out and I went flying over the bonnet of the car like a Lycra-clad Lucha Libre. I took her number plate and phone number and told her not to worry. Apart from a cut hand, I was fine. More importantly, my bike was unscathed.

I waved her off and continued riding to work. It was only then that the pain started. Every time I breathed in, I felt a pain in my ribs. So I slowly carried on riding to work, being overtaken by old ladies and girls on bikes with baskets. At one point, I swore I saw a snail overtake me.

I finally got to work after what seemed like an eternity, and told the PA what had happened. She instantly booked me a doctor's appointment for an hour's time.

The doctor said it wasn't too serious. It just looked like I'd badly bruised my ribs. The only advice he gave was to try not to sneeze and to avoid laughing. As as long I didn't get hay fever at a comedy club, I should be fine!

I was sore for a few weeks but I was soon back in full training for the forthcoming London Triathlon. I would be racing Mark again, so I'd want to be as fit as possible.

Try Tri Again

THE run-up to the race had gone fairly smoothly after my ribs healed. My running was getting better, cycling was good and my swimming, well, it hadn't got any worse.

Mark and I would be racing in the same wave, so the stage was set. We met up with Mark and Zoe in the huge cavernous building that houses the car park at London's Excel, where the race started.

We were lucky: it was another bright, sunny day. Three races, three lots of decent weather. One of the worst things about racing in the UK was the weather. But so far, I'd been lucky (I wouldn't always be so lucky, but I'll tell you about that later.)

The other great thing about this race was that I'd contacted the organisers and requested a 2pm start, so there was no need to get up in the middle of the night to force-feed myself dry, burnt bagels. It was all shaping up to be a great race.

As I proudly wandered around in my Windsor Triathlon T-shirt, I noticed the guy next to me had an Ironman 70.3 T-Shirt on. I chatted to him briefly about it. He seemed a bit overweight to be racing this distance and he had a normal road bike, not some space-age carbon razor blade. Maybe this wasn't so far out of my reach after all. I mean, if a 'normal' guy like him could do it, maybe I could give it a go.

As I thought about this, the announcer started calling us to the start. I wasn't nervous this time, I knew what to expect. I had a race plan. I'd even bought a Garmin GPS watch, so I could see how fast (or slow) I'd be going and could pace myself.

We paddled out to the starting line and it was reassuring to see plenty of people beginning to panic. Nothing settles your mind like seeing other people out of control when you know what you're doing.

On the left-hand side were the yellow buoys. They were held together by yellow rope. I thought if I stick near these, I could follow it while swimming the quickest route to the turning point. There was a bit of a fight at the beginning but nothing like last time. In fact, this time I was actually swimming over people, not on purpose, but it's understood that at the beginning of a race it's every man for himself.

I got to the turning point and practised my back turn, which should enable me to go effortlessly around the buoy without missing a stroke. I made a right dog's dinner of this and took in a huge mouthful of water. Coughing and spluttering, I realised that I wasn't quite the professional I thought I was. That'll teach me.

But still, I looked at my watch and it had only taken 14 minutes something, so if I could carry on at this pace I'd beat my old swim time. Head down, I pushed on. As I go closer to the jetty, I kicked my legs hard. I'd read that when you swim, all the blood rushes to the top of your body. So by kicking more as you reach the finish, it stops you getting light headed. I climbed up the steps to find it had worked. I looked at my watch and I'd beat my last time by over two minutes.

I quickly slipped out of my wetsuit, chucked it into the bag and sprinted towards transition. I'd 'accidently' spilt talcum powder all over the floor near my bike, so it would be easy to find.

My bike shoes were already clipped into my pedals, so I could pedal off with my feet over my shoes and then do them up when I was moving, saving me more time. I headed out on to the bike feeling good. It was quite windy but not too bad.

Unlike last time, I overtook quite a lot of people. Then, suddenly, everything slowed down and I could see blue flashing lights. A guy had come off his bike and was lying by the side of the road. He was being tended to by two ambulance men. It looked pretty nasty. There was a lot of blood. I hoped he was all right.

As I biked back down the road, I saw Mark coming the other way. In my head, I tried to work out how far ahead I was. I've often tried to work out times, speeds etc, while riding/running flat out. But the blood must rush everywhere but the brain because simple sums become almost impossible.

I kept going, knowing that the only chance I had was to get ahead of Mark on the bike. But he had a new bike and had been cycling more, so he wasn't far behind.

I could know see the Excel Centre coming into view. I lowered myself and pedalled flat out, remembering just in time to spin a smaller gear as I neared the finish. The point of this is to get your legs ready for the lung-busting run. But I knew it would still hurt like hell.

I racked my bike and jogged off out on to the run course. It was four laps, 2.5km each. It doesn't sound like much but it felt like miles – and I was currently running like I'd just graduated from the ministry of silly walks.

At each aid station, I tried to get a drink of Powerade. As I tried to drink and run, I saw Mark run past me in the opposite direction. All I could manage was a pained smile. I was too tired to care how close he was to me, so I just pushed on.

On the final lap, I could see I was going to beat my old time and I'd beat it by at least 15 minutes. I'd go under two hours 30 minutes, provided I didn't collapse. With one kilometre to go, I started to try and speed up. It was beginning to hurt. This is when it becomes mind over matter. The body would give up if it had a choice but one tiny, sadistic part of the brain pushes you on.

All of a sudden, I felt a pinch in my left butt cheek. It was Mark. 'You alright?' he casually said as he ran past me. 'Come on.' I tried to keep up with him but he slowly left me behind. Git.

I sprinted through the tunnel of people that leads to the finish. I looked at my watch and I'd beaten my old time by 17 minutes. I bent over gasping for breath, wretched, and nearly threw up over a small child. But luckily for him, I didn't coat him in second-hand energy drink as nothing came up. I saw Mark and congratulated him. It was PBs for both of us, so we were both pretty chuffed.

We went off to find our long-suffering girlfriends, the unsung heroes of every race. In fact, any wife or girlfriend (or husband or boyfriend) who supports their other halves, they're the ones who *really* deserve the medals.

On TV, you get to watch the entire race. But as a spectator you see the person racing fly past, then wait for about an hour to see them again. I often asked Julie how she dealt with the boredom. She pointed out that it wasn't such a struggle to stand around watching fit men with, in her words, 'tight buns'. I guess it was the equivalent of me watching a beach volleyball match.

After all that exercise, it was time to find something to eat. We found a bar and recovered like many a professional athlete, with a pint of Strongbow and a burger, with cheese, extra bacon, barbecue sauce and chips.

I wolfed down my food like a hungry Labrador eating chocolate cake. Then Mark had a bit of a funny turn. It had been pretty hot out on the course and we were now feeling it. But it was nothing a packet of beef Monster Munch wouldn't sort out. Who needs SiS recovery shakes when you've got beef-flavoured maize snacks?

Mark recovered and we said goodbye before Julie drove me home. As we headed out of the car park, a huge dark cloud rolled in and it suddenly went very dark. The heavens opened. I could see people still out on the course racing. It very quickly went from being a nice day to armageddon. I was glad to be leaving. On the whole, it had been another great race. But what next? A half-ironman seemed like the next logical step. After speaking to that guy at the start, it seemed well within my grasp.

The swim was 1.9km, only 400m longer than the swim I'd just done. The bike was double an Olympic distance (plus 10km) and a half-marathon was doable. But before I gave this any more thought, I'd have another visit to the hospital.

Can I? Should I?

INSTEAD of heading to my usual room in a London Bridge hospital, the receptionist informed me that I was to go to the other side of the building because some construction work was being done. As I wandered over to find where I was supposed to be, my thoughts started racing. They always did when I got to the hospital. It made my illness suddenly very real again.

I was feeling good after my races but I was still really worried about this result. I was fitter than I'd ever been in my entire life, yet I was also ill. I hated the fact I was ill. Why me? There are loads of people out there who don't take care of themselves. They smoke, they drink too much. Every day, I see more and more obese people stuffing themselves with junk, without a care in the world. They're the ones who should get ill. Not me.

If they knew what it was like to be ill, they wouldn't be like that. Why me? It made me so fucking angry. Everything had changed, yet nothing had. I was ill but I felt fine. Maybe there'd been a mistake. Perhaps the blood test was wrong. I was probably going to be one of the lucky ones who outlived the illness, before it damaged my kidneys, so I wouldn't have to go dialysis.

As I walked over the walkway, with these thoughts bouncing around my head, I saw a door that was open. Inside, there was huge machine that was switched on, making a beeping sound. Being generally nosey and quite curious, I peered in. There was a guy hooked up to a dialysis machine. I'd seen these on the internet. But never for real.

The guy lying in the bed was asleep. He looked ill. Really ill. He was this horrible yellowy, grey colour. He had two large tubes plugged into his chest. It looked like blood was coming out of the tubes and going into the machine. So, this was dialysis. It looked worse than I'd imagined. It wasn't so much the blood. I'm not squeamish at all. It was how ill he looked that worried me.

He was very old, admittedly, but he looked totally lifeless. It was like the machine was sucking the life out of him. Ironically, it was doing exactly the opposite. Someone with kidney failure can't survive many months without it. It was actually keeping him alive.

The machine acts like a mechanical kidney. It 'cleans' the blood by removing all the waste products your body doesn't need. But unfortunately, it can only do the job of a kidney working between eight and ten per cent. Just enough to keep you alive.

This couldn't happen to me? Could it? No, I'd probably be fine. But the doctor said sometimes, with the disease I've got, it accelerates quickly. So it could. Couldn't it? Maybe.

Just as my minded started racing again, a nurse walked down the corridor and I quickly pretended I was looking for something. I asked where the doctors were today and she pointed towards the waiting room.

Waiting here was the most worried I'd ever been. At least I would be seeing the doctor in a few minutes. I wouldn't have long to sit around stewing about it. I could ask him how long he thought my kidneys would last. Hopefully, he could put my mind at rest. I also wanted to ask him if he thought I'd be capable of doing a half-Ironman.

I wanted to prove to myself that I wasn't sick. I was fit but I hadn't completely lost my mind. I didn't want to die doing it. That would kind of defeat the object. As I sat in the waiting room flicking through *GQ* (no tea or biscuits this time), the door opened and Dr Abbs, my doctor, called my name.

I sat down and the first thing he asked me was how many races had I done. He asked a surprising amount of questions about triathlon. He was asking how much I trained, where I'd bought my wetsuit and which race I had enjoyed the most. I found out why when he told me he was thinking of entering one himself as he felt he needed to get fit.

I answered his questions and shared my limited knowledge with him. He seemed interested. I also asked if he thought it would be possible for me to race the longer distance. He said if I was considering swimming 2km, cycling 90km and then running half a marathon for fun, it wasn't my kidneys I needed to worry about but my brain. He chuckled to himself, sounding like the doctor from *The Simpsons*.

He did say that if I did it, I should be very careful about hydration. If I got badly dehydrated, it could finish my kidneys completely. He also said that while my kidneys were relatively stable at the moment, the potassium in my blood was a little high. So I should avoid drinking fresh orange juice and not eat too many bananas. I drank fresh juice by the bucket load, so much so that me giving it up would probably affect the man from Del Monte's profit margins. He'd no longer be saying 'Yes', he'd be saying, 'Hello, is that *Wonga. com?*

This was the first real symptom I'd experienced with the disease. It didn't sound like much but high potassium can cause heart attacks. It wasn't that high. But it certainly wasn't good news. I decided to ask him how long he thought I had. He gave me the typical doctor's answer, which was neither good nor bad. In truth, he didn't know. That's the trouble with IgA nephropathy. It's so variable.

He reassured me again that I'd probably be fine to race and he thought I should go for it. He just reiterated that I shouldn't get dehydrated. He also followed this up by telling me that I shouldn't over-hydrate either. This can actually be more dangerous.

There was now nothing to stop me stepping up to the half-Ironman distance now the doctor had given me the OK. All I had to do was choose a race. Ironman wasn't as big as it is now. But there was still a hell of a lot of places to choose from. Everywhere from Brazil to Thailand.

There were also loads of other races that weren't Ironman 'branded' races. Working in advertising I should know that a brand is just that. It rarely makes much difference to the actual product. It wouldn't make much difference to how I raced. It was the distance that really mattered. But Ironman did sound cooler. Plus, it was the original.

Thinking back to what the doctor had told me, I decided against Thailand, Brazil or anywhere where I'd have to race in ridiculous temperatures. I had no intention of finishing the race looking like a human sultana, or on a drip in the finishers' tent. So it would probably be a good idea to stay in the UK to race. Besides, if anything went wrong, I'd be closer to a decent hospital.

The UK Ironman 70.3 (the numbers represent the total number of miles you race) was in an area called Wimpleball, in Exmoor. It had been going for years. In fact, it was one of the first 'half'-Ironman events. Perfect. It wouldn't be too hot and I could drive, which meant I wouldn't have the hassle of taking my bike apart and transporting it in a bike box. It would be hard enough as it was without my bike falling to pieces halfway through the course. Plus, a few guys at the club had done it, so they could give me advice.

I went on to the web page, entered my details and paid. There was no hesitation this time. I wanted to do it. I'd gone from being nervous and a little unsure about racing to loving it. I actually missed it when I couldn't train. It made me feel better than I ever have.

Without really realising it, my body and energy levels had completely changed. I was never fat enough to be on a

Channel 5 documentary but I'd gone from 13 stone to 11 3/4. My clothes fitted better. I was never tired. I could happily get up early, go for a run, come back and have breakfast before going to work. I had gone, as my mates regularly told me, properly mental. After work, I'd actually want to go swimming. I rarely watched evening TV any more and Julie was quite happy not to have me moaning all the way through *EastEnders* and *Coronation Street*. I also saved a fortune on travel to work by commuting on my bike.

I couldn't wait to go on the usual Saturday ride with the club to pick their brains on what I should do and how I should start training. I turned up at the usual meeting point and asked what it was like and when I should start training. The first question someone asked me was, 'Do you like hills?'

'Erm... why?' I replied.

'Wimpleball is one of the hardest half Ironman courses there is. The bike has over 1,190m of climbing. But the run is where it really hurts.'

Oh good, so unbeknown to me I'd inadvertently entered one of the toughest races at this distance in my first race. Bugger. On the bright side, at least if I ever did another one, I could pick a flatter one and get a better time.

After the ride, I looked up the course to see what I was letting myself in for. There was a quote on the web page from last year's winner saying it was 'one of the toughest courses on the circuit.' In my excitement, I must have missed this. I also checked the course. Sure enough, the bike was very hilly and so was the run.

I didn't really know what 1,100m of climbing would be like on a bike. The closest thing I could compare it to was the total ascent of the Alpe d'Huez, one of the famous mountain stages at the Tour de France.

While I was in the mood for booking things, I decided to book a Christmas break in New York. Not only would I surprise Julie with this early Christmas present, I'd also find somewhere where I could pop the question.

A Decent Proposal

THERE was still a few weeks before we were due to fly and Julie still had no idea we were going away. However, it wouldn't remain a secret for much longer.

I was chatting to one of my mates who lives in New Zealand on e-mail. A few days later, I commented on one of his photos on Facebook. He replied and signed off with 'Enjoy NYC at Xmas, you big poof'. I'd told him about my romantic plans and this was his way of saying he hoped it went well, and what a nice idea it was.

Thanks to this comment, Julie saw it, put two and two together and came up with 'woo hoo! we're going to New York for Christmas.' So I told her we'd be flying out on Christmas Day and coming home on New Year's Eve. But the bit she didn't know about was my plan to propose.

According to the weather report, it was about -5, so I packed everything I owned and Julie did the same. But then she always did. She liked, as she would say, to be able to choose what to wear when she got there. This would have been fine but her case usually ended up so heavy that she couldn't lift it. So I'd have to carry it.

We set off early on Christmas Day. Not surprisingly, the roads were empty. It was quite eerie. When we arrived at

Gatwick, it was chaos. Because it was Christmas, everyone was laden down with presents. Everyone was unpacking and repacking their suitcases trying to balance their luggage, so as not to be over the all-important weight restriction.

One woman weighed her case and the guy behind the desk told her she was 5kg over. She unzipped her case, took out a pair of flip-flops and moved them into another case, before weighing it again. Unless she wore lead flip-flops, this was going to make hardly any difference at all. This was going to take forever. But slowly we moved forward, until we were ready to check in.

A big American guy in the queue next to us lost his temper and started taking all his clothes out of his case before putting them on. I watched him put on a couple of T-shirts, two jumpers and a hat. 'Is this better?' he shouted at the check-in girl. 'Is this what its come to?' Her expression stayed blank. Thankfully, our cases were OK. So we picked up our tickets and headed off to the departure lounge to have the obligatory 'pre-holiday' full English breakfast.

I'd been to New York before but years ago and with barely any money. I'd won a trip there with Al, my art director from work. It was for Best Young Achievers at the Yorkshire Press Advertising Association Awards (a bit like the Oscars, except for regional press adverts, not blockbuster movies. Instead of Hollywood A-listers, there were lots of drunk Yorkshiremen who wanted to fight you.)

Along with the trip, we were both given $500 each spending money. We spent all of this in the first two days. The rest of our time was spent playing the pinball machine in the reception of our hotel, hanging out with a security guard who said he'd shot his brother. We also later found out that we weren't actually staying in The Big Apple at all. We were in New Jersey. It was the equivalent of winning a trip to London and then staying in Croydon.

But this time, I'd made sure we were staying in Manhattan. We landed at JFK Airport and hailed a taxi to our hotel. The driver dropped us off and swore at me for not giving him a big enough tip. I thought it was quite generous but he obviously thought otherwise. Welcome to America.

We checked in and got the lift up to our cupboard, sorry, room. It was tiny, even by New York standards. It was like a giant 3D Tetris puzzle. Everything had to be in exactly the right place or it didn't fit. But downstairs, the bar was cool. The staff couldn't do enough to help us, and it was in a great location. Besides, we hadn't come to one of the most exciting cities on earth to spend it sitting in a hotel room.

The next day, we got up and did some of the usual touristy stuff. Much to Julie's delight, I found a bike shop. I spent as much time in there as I dared before we went back to our exploring. We went up the Rockwell Centre, wandered around China Town, soaked up some culture in the MOMA (Museum of Modern Art) and had Korean soup for lunch. Julie said we'd better get back to the hotel to book somewhere to eat later. But I told her not to worry as I'd already sorted it. It was going to be a surprise.

Before we left the UK, I'd booked a meal in a pub (well, they called it a pub on their website but it was more of restaurant) called the Spotted Pig, in Greenwich Village. Julie is Chinese and her favourite food is pork, which we ate a lot. I'm probably the only triathlete who regularly eats belly pork, crackling and pork ribs. If I hadn't discovered triathlon, I'd be big enough to be hired out for kids' parties as a bouncy castle.

We arrived and there was a queue of people waiting for spare tables. Good job I booked as popping the question while kneeling in a gutter, by a bin, wouldn't quite have the romantic effect I was after. The guy on the door checked our names and a rather camp-looking manager came over and showed us to our table.

We sat down at a small candle-lit table. I decided that now was the time to ask. I'd just plucked up the courage when a waiter named Chad came over and interrupted me to announce to us that he'd be our waiter. He gave us some menus and disappeared.

'Julie...' He interrupted us again to give us some water.

We chatted for bit and I waited for a break in the conversation so I could ask her. We stopped talking and I took Julie's hand... and lo and behold, Chad appeared again.

Fourth time lucky, I asked and she said yes. Then she burst into tears. I still like to think that she was overwhelmed with happiness and not desperately depressed about spending her life with a slightly damaged amateur triathlete who got excited by expensive bikes and wetsuits.

We ate and drank into the early hours, thoroughly testing the theory that New York is the city that never sleeps. After a long night, I can safely say that it doesn't. But we needed to, so we called it a day at, well, I've no idea what time we made it back to the hotel because my memory is bit blurry, to say the least. I don't know what happened when we got back, but the next morning the receptionist asked if we enjoyed our night out because it had certainly looked like it. Another of the receptionists stifled a laugh and scurried off out the back.

I'd popped the question on our first night there so we could enjoy the rest of our time together as an engaged couple. We spent most of the time eating and drinking. We went to a very fancy three Michelin Star restaurant called Per Se, overlooking Central Park. This was as posh as it got. I even wore a suit.

We had the tasting menu, which had about nine courses. Each course came with a glass of wine to match. We were there for hours. It started as a sophisticated, fine dining experience but ended with me tripping over a rug on the way out and nearly taking out a shelf of vases that were on display. In my eyes, I'd arrived looking and feeling like James Bond but I'd left with all the style and panache of Frank Spencer. It cost a small fortune but it's not every day you get engaged.

Another meal we had was at a place called Carnegies Deli. It was famous for making huge pastrami sandwiches. It was very touristy but it was a bit like going to England and not having fish and chips. So we ordered and waited. The portions were comically big. We barely made a dent in them. But we hate wasting food, so we took the rest of it away with us. We had more as our evening meal. Later, we went out for drinks in the Meat Packing District and I came back hungry, so ate some more. The next morning, with the whole room stinking of pastrami, I finally gave in and chucked the rest away. Even then, there was still quite bit left.

Each day, we seemed to find a new way to test the buttons on our trousers. New York had every type of food you could possibly imagine. No amount of sightseeing would burn off the calories I was consuming. At this rate, I'd have to check myself in as excess baggage at the airport and be stuffed into the hold.

As the trip came to an end, I started to think about the race I had coming up. So at JFK Airport on the way home, I had a salad. I like to think this readdressed the balance. Six days stuffing my face like a gluttonous Roman emperor followed by a single salad. I boarded the plane home on New Year's Eve with my now fiancé and, despite kidney failure never being too far from my thoughts, I was happy and content.

Back in Training

MY year was set. While we started planning the wedding for July, I would also start training for my first half-Ironman in June. One would prove to be much easier than the other.

I did a bit more research this time and found a comprehensive training programme online. It started surprisingly easily. I would actually be stepping down my training. But it would soon ramp up as the weeks went by. The final long week would be 13 hours in total. As I read more on what I should achieve as I went through the programme, I noticed that I hadn't really been training properly at all. All my current training was done at the same pace. There was no variety and no strength sessions.

Until now, I just swam the distance I was due to race, twice a week. Each time, I would try and go faster. I'd never really given my technique any thought at all and the idea of breaking the swim into different lengths and speeds hadn't even crossed my mind.

It said swimming is all technique. If you have a bad technique, you can swim ten hours a week. But you wouldn't get any faster. Hmmm... I'd been going about it completely wrong. It was a relief to be honest because I'd been swimming for around two years now and I wasn't really getting any faster.

The other thing I'd have to work on would be nutrition. Racing for six-odd hours would be very different from 2½.

It also had a much more detailed cycling programme. I wouldn't just go out and ride as fast I could for a couple of hours. There was much more structure. It also suggested that I bought an indoor bike trainer called a turbo. I'd hook the bike up to this and then ride at set heart rates.

Following this new programme would mean that I'd have to do one long, easy ride a week and two sessions on the turbo.

The running training would be different as well. It would be mixed between one long, slow session and one short, fast session. Up until this point, I'd only done fast sessions, just trying to go faster each time. So apart from training badly in running, swimming, cycling and pretty much ignoring my nutrition, I knew exactly what I was doing.

As the months passed, I noticed I was slowly getting better. I'd been for swimming lessons and I was getting faster. But more importantly, it felt easier, less like I was fighting the water and more like I was gliding through it. I was also running further than I had ever run in my life.

I'd recently run a half-marathon and although the time was deeply unimpressive (one hour 45 minutes), I'd learnt that I'd have to greatly improve my pacing. I went out incredibly slowly and finished the second half of the race seven minutes quicker. But, as the say, you learn more when things go wrong.

My cycling was slowly coming on. I was now riding for around four hours every Saturday. You can cover a surprisingly long distance in this time on a bike, around 100km. So you had to make sure nothing was likely to go wrong with your bike because, if it did, it was an incredibly long walk home.

I'd started riding alone now, too, because it was easier to ride at my own pace. With the club, I'd either end up going too fast or too slow. Plus, I didn't have to stop to wait for anyone. Club riding was more sociable but when the season started properly a lot of people went out riding on their own, especially for the longer distances. It prepares you mentally as much as anything else.

One Sunday, I got up early and set off in my usual direction towards the North Downs, through the rather odd-named villages that populate the Kent countryside. Up the hill to Wittering Shit, over the bridge into Sweaty Jessop and down the valley before going up into Pratt's Bottom. (Just to prove my point, one of these names is actually a village.) It was a warm spring day and there wasn't a cloud in the sky. Perfect – although this was about to change.

As I reached about 50km (about 30miles in old money) from home, I started to work out how to get back home. I never really knew where I was going and rarely bothered to have a planned route. If I reached the sea, I knew I'd gone too far and it was time to turn around. It was pretty much that simple.

As I turned back to ride up the hill I'd just come down, my chain suddenly snapped. I was miles from anywhere. I reached for my mobile but it wasn't there. I must have left it on the kitchen table when I left.

I started to walk back towards the last village I'd just come through. As I walked, I noticed a horrible smell. I looked down at my bike shoe. I'd stepped in some kind of animal shit, dog probably. Could today get any worse?

After cleaning my shoes and walking for about 40 minutes, I came across a village shop. Of course, it was closed. A little further down the road, I could see a pub that would be open. I could go in there, call a taxi and get back home. Failing that, I could go full Ray Mears, build a lean-to out of sticks and live on a diet of badger that I could trap using my limited bush craft skills.

As I neared the pub, I started to visualise what the locals might be like inside. It looked a bit creepy. Just then, right on cue, a large black crow flew by squawking. I started to imagine that it would be like *The Slaughtered Lamb* in the film *An American Werewolf in London*. As I walked in dressed from head to toe in black lycra, looking like a portly ninja, the entire pub would fall silent and stare at me.

I cautiously walked into the pub and the door slowly creaked open. Surprisingly, I wasn't stonewalled by a mob of angry farmers with pitchforks. It was the exact opposite. I went in and asked the landlord if I could borrow his phone to call a taxi to pick me up. After I'd explained what had happened, an old guy said rather than me spending a fortune on a taxi back to south-east London, he could give me a lift to the station (or he might murder me and dump me in a bush). Luckily, it turned out to be the former.

I thanked him and took him up on his offer. He helped me load my bike into his car and off we went. He was quite shocked when I told him where I lived. Most people who don't ride are surprised how far the average weekend amateur cyclist goes. But for other cyclists, a four-hour ride on a Saturday is pretty average.

He dropped me off at the station, I thanked him and went off to find a train that would get me back to London. It took me about 90 minutes to get home because I had to change trains twice. Still, lesson learnt. I'd check my bike thoroughly before I went out from now on. And I'd take much better care of it, getting it serviced a couple of times a year.

My bike wasn't the only thing that needed to be regularly checked. It was check-up time again and I was only a month away from the race. I didn't feel any different. So I was hoping for good news.

Back to the Doctor's

I AWOKE early and got into my bike gear and cycled off to London Bridge hospital. I always biked into hospital and then into work. It made me feel better. I couldn't be that ill if I could easily cycle the 12 miles from home to the hospital and then to work. It was like a front I put up for myself. While I was training, I was well.

Being known as the guy who does triathlons made the whole thing easier to handle. I don't really know why. I think at this stage of my illness I was still in denial, which is one of the many stages you go through when you discover you're ill.

It is similar to dealing with grief. First, there's denial and isolation, feeling like you're the only person dealing with it.

Then comes the anger, which I'd already experienced.

Next comes the bargaining. You start thinking that maybe there has been a mistake, or perhaps you'll get better.

Then, depression. This is the only emotion I hadn't had yet. I was an incredibly positive person and my training was helping me deal with it as much mentally as it was physically.

Other people say brave. But I don't believe this at all. It's just something you have to deal with. You don't have a choice. 'Brave' is something 'well' people say just because you don't spend your entire time crying and moaning about it.

And finally, you experience acceptance. The worst has happened and you just get on with it. Well, what else are you going to do?

I went in to see the nurse for my blood test and blood pressure check. Instead of waiting a couple of days for the results, they now sent the bloods straight to the lab and I'd see the doctor about an hour later. I waited patiently outside the doctor's door waiting to be called.

Mr Driver? I went inside and he asked how I was. I said that I was kind of hoping he could tell me that. He smiled and flicked through the results. 'Hmmmm,' he said. And then he didn't say anything for what seemed like an eternity. It was like when they read the results on those talent contests on TV, although I'm sure he wasn't doing it for dramatic effect.

He told me that it wasn't great news. My Creatinine had gone up to 189. This meant I was now classed as a stage 3 kidney disease patient.

I questioned what this meant and he said it meant nothing really. It's just brackets that medical professionals put the results into. I shouldn't worry too much if I felt OK. But he did say I might start experiencing some of the symptoms of kidney failure.

They'd have to watch my potassium and phosphate levels. Potassium, as I've already explained, can affect heart rhythm, which in serious cases can be fatal. High levels of phosphate can cause bone disease. But hey, apart from brittle bones and heart attacks, I had nothing to worry about. He gave me a prescription for some pills to help keep my phospahte low and told me that it wasn't dangerously high. But we'd need to keep an eye on it.

He went on to enquire if any of my family were the same blood group as me and did I have any brothers or sisters? He also asked if I'd spoken to them about the possibility of them donating?

At this stage I hadn't but he suggested that I do so. He said that it could take some people a long time to come round to the idea, while others would offer to be a donor straight away. There was even a chance they could refuse. He said it's highly unlikely for families not to help out other family members. But I should be ready in case they did. (I didn't think this would be the case, as I like to think were close. And I'd definitely do it for one of them).

He followed up by saying that he didn't want me to worry as it looked like my kidneys would hold out for a good while yet. But it's not the kind of thing you leave to the last minute.

He wished me good luck for the race and said that I should now come back every two months for check-ups.

The First of Many

I NOW only had a few weeks until the race. This meant it was time to start tapering, so my body would have time to recover and repair itself before the race. I was tempted to go further for longer but I stuck to the programme until it was time to race.

Unfortunately, Julie wouldn't be coming with me because it clashed with her cousin's wedding. Obviously, this made me incredibly popular. She'd already put up with a lot but to be fair this was the first time I'd missed anything important.

There was a guy called John I knew from the club who was going to be camping at the venue. So the plan was to go up, stay somewhere local and then call John after the race so we could meet up. Plus, one of my oldest mates, Phil, had agreed to come with me. So I wouldn't be going alone.

I'd already booked a double room at a local pub that was close(ish) to where I'd race. But now I would be sharing a room with Phil, and not Julie, I had to put in an urgent call to the pub to make sure there were two beds.

Luckily, they said it was fine. I'm sure this was as much a relief for Phil as it was for me. They also said they'd put on an early breakfast from 4am, so all the athletes could eat before heading over to the venue.

I'd booked the Friday off so I could head down to Exmoor, where the race was, during the day and meet Phil in the evening. We could go out for a few pints (well, one shandy for me) then on Saturday we could check out the swim, bike and run course.

I kissed Julie goodbye and headed off. As I got closer to the venue, I started to see more and more cars with bikes on the back. By the time I arrived, there were athletes everywhere. Some were running, some were putting their bikes together. Others were just hanging around chatting. It looked like the quiet little town had been completely taken over by triathletes.

I found a car park and started to unpack my stuff. I unloaded all my race stuff and started looking for my bag with all my other clothes in. But I couldn't find it anywhere. I'd concentrated so hard on not leaving behind any of my racing stuff that I'd left my other bag behind. I called Julie and she answered the phone with a resigned 'Yesss...'

She already knew what I was going to ask her. And she sarcastically asked me if I'd forgotten something – like all my clothes, my wash bag and my pills.

Great. I was about to do my longest race ever, with stage 3 kidney disease, and I'd left my blood pressure pills behind. Panicking, I called a 24-hour doctor and asked him what I should do. Would it be OK to race? Please don't tell me I've got to go all the way home (four hours there, four hours back) to pick them up. Thankfully, he said no such thing. He told me that my blood pressure would be all over the place during the race and missing them for a couple of days would really make no difference.

I thanked him and headed off to find a local pharmacy so I could stock up on shower gel, toothpaste, a toothbrush and all the stuff I'd left behind. I also bought four bottles of Lucozade Sport to fill my bike bottles with. I had to make sure I stayed fully hydrated over the next couple of days so I'd be ready to race on Sunday.

Phil arrived at the pub and I helped him unload his stuff. He'd brought his bike, too, so he could do some of the course on Saturday.

We then went downstairs to the bar. It was getting busy now because the World Cup was on and England were playing. This made for a desperately boring spectacle at the best of times but watching it without beer made it even more tedious.

I was also trying to eat nothing too heavy. Phil had a delicious-looking pie, made by a local butcher, with lashings of thick beef and onion gravy. I had some rather odd looking salmon pasta (I think) with a sprinkling of parsley. But what did I expect in a Somerset pub that was usually full of farmers? The pies were always going to be good. The pasta, less so.

We watched (slept) through the football and went to bed around 11pm. Luckily, they'd remembered my request and we dozed off in our separate beds.

The next morning, we got up and the sun didn't just have his hat on, he had his shades, his flip-flops and a liberal helping of Factor 50. It was glorious. I hoped it would stay like this until Sunday. It would be perfect race conditions. I'd been incredibly lucky with the weather at my races and it looked like this luck was going to continue.

I'd brought my satnav, so I could drive to the venue and use it to memorise the directions. I tried putting in the postcode to the venue but the map that came up was trying to send me to somewhere in Scotland, which wasn't very helpful. But there were loads of other people driving to the venue, so I just followed them.

I pulled up at the venue and joined all the others getting ready. The idea was to sign in, rack my bike and sort out transition. Then I'd have a quick swim to get my bearings and check out the start. After that, we'd go for a spin on our bikes.

Unlike the London races I'd done, there were a lot more, what I'd call, proper-looking athletes here. There were people from all over the world. Plus, there were all the elite athletes that raced for a living. TV crews were dotted around interviewing them. How would they race? Were they in good form coming into the race? I hung around watching. Needless to say, no one asked me any such questions.

Just then, a guy with a microphone came over to me. Did he want to know what form I was in? Perhaps he wanted to know what my tactics for the race would be? No, he asked me if I knew where the portaloos were.

As I looked around, it dawned on me that this was the real deal. There weren't many first-timers here. I'll be honest, it scared the crap out of me. But in a good way. I felt very out of my comfort zone – but I loved it.

After signing in, I put on my wetsuit and headed down to the water. It was cold but the buoys were clearly visible, so it would be easy to see the route. Well, it was without any other swimmers there anyway. In the back of my mind, I was still aware that the bike course was supposed to be the 'hardest' on the circuit. As we biked to the beginning of the course, it didn't disappoint. It was incredibly hilly. There weren't many flat bits at all. But I wasn't too worried. Like I said, this was my first race at this distance, so the aim was to finish in one piece, alive.

We had a quick look around the Expo event before venturing out into the Somerset countryside to find somewhere for lunch, which meant more pasta for me. Phil had a ploughman's with a fine spread of locally produced cheese and some homemade chutney. He also had a pint of Somerset Cider. Although the pasta was OK, I'd have murdered a pint and a ploughman's as we sat out in the sun.

As Phil had driven, I'd be the one who would end up driving back. It turned out the local brew Phil was drinking was about nine per cent. He was definitely getting the better deal of this little holiday. I finished my pasta and drank my coke before driving a tipsy Phil back to the pub.

Back at the pub, Phil was now well in the mood to carry on. Unfortunately I couldn't join him, as I'd be racing. We went to a few other pubs and after a while I got bored of drinking water, so we went back to the room to watch TV and relax so I could get ready for the race.

I knew I wouldn't sleep very well because I was nervous and excited. What I hadn't counted on was my 'support' snoring all night. I gave Phil a kick and he stopped. Five minutes later, he started again. Kick. Snore. Kick. Snore. This is how it continued pretty much all night. Well, I say all night. My alarm went off 4am, so I could get up and eat a healthy bowl of dust with all the other athletes.

I'd given up on bagels and now I ate muesli before each session. It's vital that as part of your training that you practice what you'll eat before the race. The day of the race isn't the time to change and experiment. If it didn't agree with you, it could ruin your race. It may not sound like a big deal but an upset stomach on the run could not only be painful, it could lead to many visits to the portaloos on the course. On a hot day, with over 1,500 other athletes racing, these were not places you'd want to spend any time.

I went back to the room and woke up Phil before we headed off. I tried the satnav but it just kept saying 'searching for route'. Phil said he could remember the way, so he'd lead and I would follow him.

About 15 minutes later, Phil indicated and pulled over. I got out and went over to see what was wrong. He couldn't remember the way after all. We still had plenty of time but with no map, no satnav and no one to ask for directions, it wasn't looking good. We turned around and headed back to where we started. Perhaps we'd just missed a turning. We soon realised this wasn't the case and we just got more lost.

I tried to get the satnav working again. But it was useless. As I sat waiting for it to find the route, a car drove past with a Cervelo P3 on the back with Zipp 404 on the front and Zipp 808 on the back (to those who aren't triathletes this translates as a show-off's bike with expensive wheels.) We both jumped into our cars with the speed and agility of Bodie and Doyle, if they'd suffered from arthritis, and followed the car. It had to be going to the race, surely.

He didn't let us down. We arrived at the venue to see hundreds of other athletes getting ready. I was wearing my tri suit under my clothes and I already had my race chip strapped to my leg. All I needed was my water bottles and food to put on the bike, and my wetsuit and goggles. My goggles... oh no. Phew, I'd put them in the arm of my wetsuit for safekeeping. My nervous excitement was making me forget stuff.

I love this part before a race. Everyone is flapping around nervously checking his or her bike, GPS watches, pedals, tyres, and food. It's already been checked a thousand times by now but there's that tiny part of your brain that tells you to check one more time. After all, most people had trained around six months for this, booked a hotel for a few days and paid the entry. Quite a few weren't from the UK either, so they had flights to add to this spiralling cost. The last thing you wanted do was leave behind a vital piece of equipment.

I checked everything, Phil wished me luck and I walked down to the start. I got into the water and made sure my wetsuit was loose in the right places. You have to get water inside your wetsuit so you can adjust it. This is cold at first but you soon warm up. I got out of the water and finished the energy drink that I'd been sipping since breakfast. I also had an energy gel before getting back into the water, ready for the off. I made sure I was at the back, on the right-hand side. This would be the shortest route, without the risk of being swum over too much.

This was the biggest group I'd swum with. I think there must have been at least 800 of us. I tried to breathe deeply and stay calm. Deep breath in and out. Focus on the first buoy and get ready to go. Five, four, three, two, one, the horn sounded and we were off.

As usual, it was chaos. Arms, legs, heads, breath, swim, foot, mouthful of water, swim, breath... but it didn't last long.

Quite quickly, I had some space and could get into swimming from buoy to buoy, ticking off the metres.

I got to the farthest point and looked at my watch. It was about 18 minutes. Not bad. I'd be happy with 36. But unlike the other distances, I had to make sure I paced myself. The bike course was supposed to be brutal and the run just as bad. So I should keep something back.

I could now hear the music, so I must be getting close. I looked up and could see the exit. My shoulders were now getting tired but I knew I could easily make it. As I got closer to the shore, one of the support crew put out a hand to help me as I staggered out of the water.

I quickly took off my goggles and swim cap and peeled off my wetsuit down to my waist, so I could run up the bank to transition, where my bike was waiting. The grassy path from the lake to my bike was uphill. I was tired already. This didn't bode well for the next six-odd hours.

I reached my bike, chucked my wetsuit in the red swim bag, slipped on my helmet, glasses and bike shoes and headed off on to the bike course.

As you get out of transition on your bike, there's a set area where you can mount your bike. This is normally quite chaotic but this course started on quite a narrow country road, so it was worse than usual. I jumped on my bike, missed clipping in my pedal and banged my balls on the seat. The pain was excruciating. I was only distracted by the guy behind me falling off his bike and crashing into a bush. The sooner I got out of here, the better.

I stood up on the pedals and pushed hard to get over this first hill. I soon realised that this wasn't the type of hill you just quickly power up and over. It was a long drag. All the blood was still in my arms from the swim, so it took a little while for my legs to get going.

The bike course was seriously tough. There were 56 hills in total, which is quite something considering it's 56 miles long. Some were short and over quickly. Others took everything out of you, almost bringing you to a stop. In some cases, people stopped and pushed their bikes up the hills.

There was one hill I particularly remember. It was where everyone gathered to watch with cowbells. Just for a minute, it felt like I was summiting a climb in the Tour de France. People lined the road shouting encouragement. This gave me some extra energy. Out of the saddle I pushed up the hill, feeling strong. As soon as they were out of sight, I realised maybe this hadn't been such a good idea as my legs burned with lactic acid and my heart rate matched that of a shrew on amphetamines riding up Mont Ventoux.

I was glad I was on a road bike and not a time trial bike. A lot of the guys on the aerodynamic TT bikes were really struggling. Unless you're a strong cyclist, hilly courses are much easier on a road bike.

The good part of a riding hilly course is, obviously, what goes up must come down. I reached the peak of the hill and I was more than ready to come down. I made myself as aerodynamic as possible and tried to relax as I let myself go as fast as I dared. I picked up speed quite quickly and had to blink to keep my contact lenses in. I could feel them coming loose. I squinted harder but it was no good. One of them came out. Now I'm not blind without them but I couldn't finish the bike course at any speed without them. I still had one, though, so I could see enough.

As I continued to ride with one eye open, I realised that I'd started to go incredibly slowly. It was like I was running on empty. I looked down at the pouch on my bike where my food was and realised I was. I hadn't eaten anything.

In the excitement, my entire nutrition plan had completely gone out of the window. I only had eight miles to go and I'd barely eaten anything. I couldn't stuff myself now, either. I'd end up giving myself a stitch. I'd have to just eat a bit and hope for the best.

I cycled into transition and racked my bike, found my trainers, put on my sunglasses and sun visor and jogged off out on to the course. But my legs were gone and to make matters worse the first part of the run was another long uphill. I had no energy at all. But as usual, something in my mind forced me to keep going. As I staggered on, things started to get a bit cloudy. I was seriously suffering from lack of food. But somehow I managed to get to the first food station.

I drank two cups of flat coke, had half a banana and took two with me. Clutching them in my sweaty hands, they soon turned to mush. I ate the sickly sweet mess, sucking it off my fingers like Pooh Bear eating honey, as I focused on running. I just had to get to the next aid station. I eventually made it. I ate another banana and a gel. Slowly, I could feel myself coming back into the land of the living.

It was only now I noticed the crowds and the support. Surprisingly, there was quite a large amount of people watching and cheering us on. I pushed on, going temptingly close to the finish line. But I had another two laps to go before I'd be running down there and collecting my medal.

As I jogged on, I started to hear the crowd cheering louder. It wasn't for me. It was the pro leader from the elite woman's race. She flew past me at a blistering pace on her last lap. She was closely followed by the motorbike with a cameraman on the back.

A few seconds later, the rest of the elite women sped past me. They'd be finishing in a minute. Meanwhile, I still had a long way to go but I was feeling better. The guy in front of me I'd been following was my first target. I caught him then overtook him. I was feeling better as I slowly ticked off each mile.

I was now running, well jogging, reasonably quickly. This was still a hilly course and it hurt. But I was making progress. I knew I'd now finish. It was now just a case of how fast (or slow) it would be.

Past the finish line again, one more lap to go. I was back to the now-familiar feeling of having to dig deep. I perversely enjoy this quite dark place that you get to. It's on a completely different level but it reminds me of the scene in *Touching the Void*, where he has the song, *Brown Girl in the Ring* continually going around his head, like he's losing his mind.

In life and work, most of what you do is controlled by other people at some level. But this was all about me. If I stopped, it was my choice. If I walked, no one else would care. If I quit, no one would bat an eyelid. But it mattered to me. What I did/didn't achieve was 100 per cent down to me – and me alone. A lot of people would think, why bother? But then why bother doing anything? I think you learn a lot about yourself when you step out of your comfort zone. After all, who has a motto of 'do nothing scary, challenging or exciting in your life in case you fail?'

I stopped to take a quick pee, which was good news (although not for the spectators who were nearby). It meant I was now drinking enough that I actually had liquid to get rid of. I stretched my legs and they immediately cramped. This was my body's way of telling me it was electrolytes I needed now. I got to the next food station, grabbed some crisps (for the salt) and took two cups of electrolyte drink. I gulped it down and tried to speed up to get a half-decent time.

Surprisingly, apart from generally feeling knackered, I actually felt quite good for the last 2km. I wondered, could I double this distance and do the full event? A 3.8km swim, a 180km bike followed by a full marathon. Was this possible? Would my kidneys take it?

For the last kilometre, I ran as fast as I could. It seemed like a long time ago since I started. Well, to be precise, it was six hours, 17 minutes ago. I ran down the finishing chute as my name was read out over the speakers. I picked up an energy drink and one of the stewards put a medal around my neck and I wandered off to find my car.

I hobbled over to the car to find Phil asleep in the driving seat, covered by a copy of the *Guardian*. I laughed. 'Tired?' I enquired as I woke him up. He asked how I'd got on and after a brief chat I thanked him for coming and went off to get my bike.

Phil helped me load it on to the back of car and then he left. I got changed and settled into the driving seat for a quick sleep before calling the guy from the club so we could meet up. I'd brought a tent with me, so once I'd met up with him I could put up my tent, have a barbecue and get some rest before driving back in the morning. Well, that was the plan.

I now realised why there was no satnav signal. There was no signal of any sort in this part of the world. I called John but I couldn't get through. I had no mobile signal at all and there were thousands of people here, so I'd never find him in a million years. I decided to call it a day. It would be easier to just drive home. But as I would soon find out, driving after a race like this was anything but easy.

After about half an hour of driving my eyes started to get heavy, so I pulled over at a garage to get a couple of cans of Red Bull. I drank them down in one and continued on with my journey.

This is pretty much how the journey continued. Every hour or so, I had to stop and get more Red Bull. Then the hunger hit. I bought a sandwich then crisps and a Snickers, which I ate in the car. I then went back into the service station where I'd stopped and bought a Whopper.

Plus, I stopped at a place called Johnny Cupcakes. Odd name, I thought to myself. It sounded like a guy who had been kicked out the Mafia because he had a penchant for velour and scatter cushions. But it was, in actual fact, a place that, none too surprisingly, sold cupcakes. So I bought one of those, too.

I finished everything except the cupcake because I now felt a bit sick. I let out a huge belch, so loud that the family in the car next to me could hear me, much to the amusement of their kids. I pulled a face as if to say 'excuse me' and drove drove away.

The traffic was a nightmare. There had been an accident which had shut the motorway, so it took me about five hours to get to south-west London. My body was exhausted but my mind was wired. It was like I'd had an exercise/caffine speedball. I'd now had six cans of Red Bull to keep myself awake. At least I was now only 90 minutes away from home. The second finish line of the day was in sight.

Just as I came into Hammersmith, my satnav ran out of batteries. I know most of London, having lived there about 19 years in total. But west London was the one area that was a total mystery. So now not only was I exhausted, I was totally lost, too.

Another two hours later, I finally found myself on the Embankment, the road that runs parallel with the Thames. From here, I knew the way. I was only about 30 minutes from home.

I staggered into the house and was excitedly greeted by Julie. She gave me a funny look and asked if I was all right. She said I looked a bit 'peaky'. I told her what had happened and explained it had taken me about eight hours to get home. Plus, I had overdosed on Red Bull to stay awake, so that's probably why I looked a bit crazy. I certainly felt it. As I unloaded my race kit from the car, all the energy gel wrappers fell out of my pocket. I picked them up and noticed that these where caffeinated too. God knows how much caffeine I had coursing through my veins.

Julie had cooked lasagne, which I inhaled, before going upstairs to bed. Sitting in a car for hours hadn't done much to help my leg stiffness. It took me about another hour to get upstairs. I then spent most of the night staring at the ceiling unable to sleep. But despite all this pain and suffering, I'd loved the experience. And I knew that it wasn't going to be my last race. The question now was not could I do the full distance but when?

I Do

IN ten weeks, I was due to race the London Triathlon again. So I decided that I'd use my training for the UK Ironman 70.3 as a base and I could now just work on speed. Part of me wanted to just relax and do nothing but I was going to be racing Mark again and my competitiveness wouldn't let me give up just yet.

I found a ten-week training programme in *Triathlon Plus* and set about adding speed sessions to my plan. Halfway through this plan, I would be in Tuscany, Italy, getting married because it was where Julie and I had decided to tie the knot. Julie had contacted a wedding planner, so all we had to do was say yes or no to what they sent us. We were both quite laid back about the whole thing, so it was pretty stress free.

Do you want locally grown sunflowers, which will be much cheaper than having any other flowers? Yes.

Do you want locally sourced Italian food from the farmhouses that surround the venue? Yes.

Are you OK with wine from the vineyard where you're staying? Yes, please.

It was easy. A friend of a friend sorted Julie's and my rings. Julie had found a dress that she loved and I'd bought a suit. Everything was pretty much sorted.

We'd already been out to pick a venue and we'd found somewhere that was perfect. I'd also noticed that it would have been a great place to cycle. I would have loved to have taken my bike but I didn't even ask. If I'd come off the day before the wedding and had to get married with my face covered in road rash, Julie would never have forgiven me. Plus, no one wants to have their wedding photos retouched because they've had a bike accident and they look like a human bran flake. But when I thought about it, seriously, I realised that getting married was much more important to me than racing anyway.

We arrived at the venue and met the planners, who seemed more excited than we were. They were running around sorting out who was staying where and what time they'd be arriving. They were great. I wish I could have them all year round to just sort out my life. Nothing was too much trouble.

We unpacked and settled in as all our mates and family started to arrive. It was in the middle of nowhere, so most of them got lost. It was almost impossible to get there if you didn't have a car. I say almost, because one of mates got the train from the airport to Florence then somehow managed to get various buses, followed by a taxi, and then walked the last bit (three miles) because the taxi driver had dropped him off in the wrong village. He casually strolled into the venue and announced it had only taken five hours from the airport (by car, it was about 45 minutes).

A couple of Julie's friends phoned and said they were nearby and were excited because they could see the sea. Our venue was at least two hours from the sea. I'm amazed we didn't get married on our own. Even Julie's friend, who drove a black cab for a living, got lost.

That night, we all went out for something to eat in a local restaurant that we'd booked in advance. It was great to see everyone. I was tempted to stay out all night drinking and chatting but as we were getting married the following day we called it a day about midnight.

I woke up early the following morning and opened the shutters and breathed in deeply. I looked out over the Tuscan hills and thought to myself how lucky I was. It was one of those moments when you take time to actively try and remember how you're feeling.

I was about to get married to the woman I'd loved for 15 years. The setting was perfect. All my close friends and family were around me and I was fit and healthy. (Well, relatively healthy.) My kidneys were never far from my thoughts but today they were further than usual.

Before the ceremony, I'd wound Julie up about getting emotional. But she was OK, it was me who struggled. I'm not normally particularly emotional but today was different. I wasn't doing a Gazza but I had to do a bit of extra blinking while reading the vows.

The day flew by and everything went to plan, except for the Italian photographer. He spent most of his time eating all the food that was supposed to be for the guests, while sneakily helping himself to glass after glass of wine.

In between snaffling mini-Bruscettas, he'd get us to pose in various ridiculous ways, so he could take some photos. My favourite was a shot he composed that made it look like I was dragging Julie into a bush. David Bailey, he wasn't.

The highlight of the day for me was drinking wine while watching the sun slowly sink below the horizon of the incredible Tuscan countryside, with all my friends, family and new wife. Just when I thought things couldn't get any better, the food arrived. A slow roast, suckling pig with rosemary roast potatoes. It was a bit hot for Porchetta but it tasted delicious.

Before we went inside for the first dance, we'd had the idea to give everyone Chinese lanterns to set off. This very nearly turned into total disaster. One of the lanterns got stuck in a bracken dry tree, which caught fire. The wedding planner was running around screaming trying to get everyone to stop lighting them. But after six hours of drinking, no one was really listening. Thankfully, the rest went up without incident, the minor fire went out and the Tuscan countryside survived to see another day.

We drank and danced and drank and sang and staggered and drank into the early hours before all heading off to sleep. It had been a great day and a fantastic night. I wondered why we'd waited so long.

The next day, everyone chilled out around the pool sleeping off their hangovers. Well, I say everyone, Mark and I had decided to go for a run in the blistering Italian sun, up and down the hills. We didn't last long. Heat, hangovers and exercise don't mix. We soon gave up and went to join everyone else around the pool, just enough time for a bit of R&R before returning home.

We set off the next day with plenty of time but the traffic was terrible. It wasn't just slow, it was stationary. It was looking very likely that we'd miss the plane. Everyone in my car was getting worried, except me. I was quite happy to be stuck here for a few extra days.

Fortunately, we made it with about 20 minutes to spare. Luckily, there'd been a massive storm over northern Italy, so all the planes were delayed anyway. The airport was chaos. But eventually, we made it on board.

We landed to typical, post-holiday weather, cold, wet and grey. I had a couple of days off then it would be back to work and back in training. London was now only five weeks away. But before this, I also had another doctor's appointment.

I had my check-up and the doctor noted that my kidneys had deteriorated a bit more. Not dramatically but enough that I was now on the low side of Stage 3 kidney failure, with a creatinine of 198. My haemoglobin had also dropped to 11.5. The average healthy level for a man is between 13 and 18.

Healthy kidneys produce a hormone called erythropoietin, or EPO, which stimulates the bone marrow to produce the proper number of red blood cells needed to carry oxygen to vital organs. Diseased kidneys, however, often don't make enough EPO. As a result, the bone marrow makes fewer red blood cells, resulting in lower levels of haemoglobin. The lower it got, the more tired and out of breath I'd get. He told me that at this level he'd normally start considering EPO injections.

But considering I'd recently been training for another triathlon without any trouble, he didn't think I'd need to yet. He asked if I'd noticed any changes in how I felt. I said, weirdly, I felt great, in fact fitter than ever. He was amazed that I hadn't noticed any difference at all. He said it wasn't unusual for patients to feel OK until their kidneys were down to about 40 per cent. But none that he'd known in all his time as a doctor had been doing triathlons.

Despite what my blood results were telling me, I was more than ready to race London again. Like I've said, while I was racing and thinking about racing, I couldn't be that ill, could I? I mean, how many sick people can do triathlons?

End of the Season

I TURNED up at the Excel in London for the third time and met Mark. I was sporting my new rucksack, a 70.3 Ironman UK rucksack. I said it was a better size than my old one. But in reality everyone knew I was carrying it around to show off. Sad, I know, but at least I'm admitting it.

We registered, racked and queued up with everyone else. The race played out in similar fashion. I took the lead on the swim, rode flat out to get as far ahead of Mark as possible then try and hold on on the run.

Towards the end of the race, I saw Mark a few times. But he didn't look like he was running as fast as usual. I finished, 20 seconds slower than my PB, and Mark came in a couple of minutes behind me. He'd had stomach pains throughout the run, so hadn't been able to get up much speed. He was pretty disappointed with his run and I was pretty disappointed not to have beaten my old time.

So although technically I'd finished ahead of him, it didn't really feel like it counted. It was like winning any sporting event because of a technicality. It's not because you've performed to the best of your ability, it's because someone else hasn't. To this day, we've still got one race each. One-all.

I'd enjoyed the race but this was the third time I'd done it and a bit of the excitement had gone. The fear wasn't there any more. I knew what to expect. I needed more of a challenge now, something new. But not just yet.

After training for the half-Ironman and then London, I was ready for a rest. I'd been training pretty much solidly for the last eight months. I was now more than ready for a break.

A week or two went by and I didn't do any training. I didn't have to. I went out, drank a bit too much. (Believe it or not, drinking doesn't affect the kidneys, it's your liver that deals with that.) I had lie-ins, caught up with mates I hadn't seen for a while and generally did nothing much. But there was something missing.

Weirdly, my body still wanted to train. I thought I'd give myself four weeks of doing nothing. I had no races planned, so I should make the most of it. I was still waking up early and I still felt great but my kidneys weren't getting any better. But it wasn't until I went back to the doctor's that I realised how much worse.

I rode up to the hospital and asked the security guard if he could look after my bike as I went upstairs to see Dr Abbs. I waited outside in my usual seat. The nurse came to get me to take me for my blood test. I then hung around until the doctor called me in.

He informed me that my creatinine had risen to 210. This gave me an eGFR of just 33, which equates to about 33 per cent kidney function. He told me that we'd have to monitor it more carefully now. I should check my ankles for swelling, as kidneys also remove liquid from the blood and the more damaged they are the less liquid they'll remove. If I had any shortness of breath, I should call my GP. It was unlikely but I could get fluid on my lungs.

He also said that I should now come for check-ups every six weeks. When my kidneys had got to a stage where I'd need monthly check-ups, he'd transfer me to the renal department at Guy's Hospital. They specialised in kidney disease, transplants, transplant work-ups and what I dreaded most of all, dialysis.

My kidneys failing was now quickly becoming a reality. I still didn't really have any major symptoms and although the results sounded bad, if they kept getting worse at this rate I would actually still have a lot of time before I needed a transplant or dialysis.

By now, I'd told my family about the disease and had spoken to them about what it might mean in the future. But it still seemed like such a long way away, We'd only talked about it briefly. I hadn't actually asked outright. In fact, the only person I had asked up until now was my wife, Julie. Although hospitals terrified her, she'd already said she would be a donor.

I got home that night and called my mum and told her what stage I was at. Both she and my dad both volunteered straight away to be donors. I tried to reassure them that it wouldn't happen any day soon. But it was nice to know. Next, I'd have to speak to my brother, Mark.

I've still no idea why I did this. But I sent him an e-mail asking him, if the worst came to the worst, would he consider donating? An e-mail. Not a letter. Not a phone call. I sent him an e-mail asking if he'd put his life on the line by donating one of his kidneys to me. It's not lost on me how ridiculous this sounds now. But at the time, I think I was still so much in denial that I thought it would probably never happen.

Being the incredibly selfless guy he is, he replied straight away, saying of course he would because he's my brother and he knew I'd do the same for him. He said he didn't need to give it any thought at all. He instantly knew he'd do it.

This is an incredibly humbling e-mail to receive at work while you're trying to write adverts selling annuities to pensioners. In fact, it was hard to care about anything to do with work for the rest of the day. Obviously, life has to carry on as normal but it can be hard to take the little things in life seriously when you've got stuff like this going on in the background.

It was reassuring to know this. Obviously, my mum, dad and brother would have to go through rigorous testing. But surely one would be a match. Besides, I didn't want to even think about the alternative.

It had now been about four weeks since I'd done any real training and it didn't take my body long to get used to not getting up early and running, swimming or cycling. That's the thing with races, it gives you something to aim for. Without that goal, it was easy for me to fall out of the routine. But it had now been a month without me really doing anything and I was starting to miss it.

I gave it another two weeks before I decided to go for a run. About 25 minutes into the run, I was in agony. My ankles felt like they were on fire. I've never felt anything like it. I hobbled back home looking like John Wayne with piles. I assumed this must be somehow connected to my kidneys or the drugs I was taking had affected my tendons. I didn't really know what had caused it but whatever it was I was convinced that it meant things were getting worse.

I called Rhys, the physio I'd seen before, and made an appointment. It took him about 30 seconds to work out what was wrong. I'd been wearing the trainers I'd trained and raced in. They had seen much better days. The heel was crushed on the right side, so I'd strained all the tendons in my ankles.

While he checked me over for other strains and areas where my muscles might have been damaged, he told me that he'd signed up for Ironman Switzerland. One of his customers, a Spanish guy called Fran (short for Francisco), was training him. He said he'd never thought he'd ever be able to do it but Fran talked him through what it would actually entail. It sounded hard, but definitely doable.

I said that despite my illness I was thinking of doing the full distance next year and would be interested in catching up with Fran and having a chat, just to see if actually racing the full distance was possible. Rhys told me the first thing I should do is buy some new trainers and chuck my old ones in the bin before I did myself any more damage. He also gave me Fran's number, so I could give him a bell and we could meet up.

In my mind, I could see how this meeting would pan out. After a brief chat, I'd realise that training for an endurance event that lasts all day would be impossible for someone with a wife, a full-time job, a social life and chronic kidney disease. So I'd thank him for his time, go home and forget all about it.

The End

Thankfully this wasn't the case. Otherwise this story would come to a spectacularly underwhelming finish.

My first race. I'm the one on the right with the pink hat on.

The top of Ide Hill in Kent, one of my favourite training rides.

My first half Ironman photo which, by the look of it, was taken by a dwarf.

My love.

Going way too fast on the bike section of the Outlaw, I'd pay for this on the run.

Finishing the Outlaw, my first full Iron distance race. The smile hides the pain.

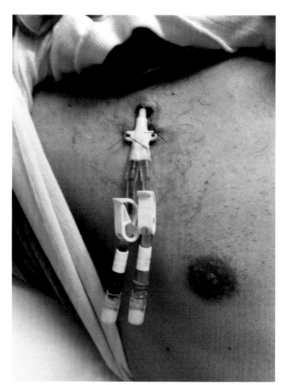

The neckline that I had to live with for five months while had I haemodialysis.

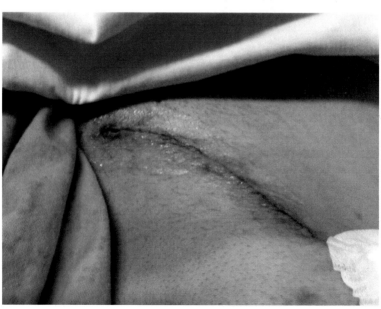

A very tidy post-operation scar, thanks to my skilled surgeon.

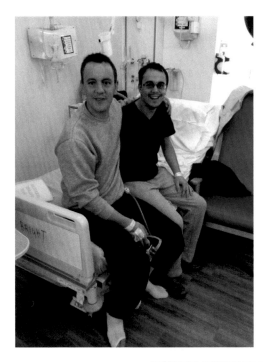

Brotherly love. Four days after the operation and Mark is getting ready to go home.

Training in the Alps, building back up to full fitness.

Exiting the swim in my comeback race.

The hills are alive with the sound of heavy breathing.

Running down the finishing chute in Germany.

Sprinting over the finish line in Germany might have saved a few seconds but it didn't make great for a great photo.

Bling

Me and my girls.

Coach Fran

I MADE my excuses and left work early. I'd arranged to see Fran at a local Starbucks near work. An odd choice for me because I despised coffee. I've no idea why. I hated the smell and I hated the taste. But it seemed like an appropriate place. I toyed with the idea of meeting in a pub, but greeting my new coach with a pint of beer and a packet of pork scratchings might not be the best start.

I arrived early, with all my last year's training printed out. I had a record of all my times to date, too. As I stood at the counter trying to find something to order that wasn't coffee, a Spanish guy in a running top came in and ordered an espresso. Fran?

He greeted me and we sat down. Fran briefly told me his training history as a personal trainer and how he could help me. He talked in general about what it takes. Surprisingly, it sounded achievable and not just for super-fit professional athletes. Doable for an average Joe, like me. Even with dodgy kidneys.

He told me the big mistake most first-time Ironman athletes make is to sign up, then go crazy, putting in hours and hours of training. He explained that it took a long time to build up to race distances. If I decided to join him, I would follow a ten-month plan, including weekly strength sessions. I'd also need to get a bike fit, along with swim training, a review of my nutrition, a full check-up by a physio and consultation with a podiatrist to make sure I bought the right running shoes.

What I liked about him was that he didn't say any of this was vital but the chances are it would save me getting injured further into the programme. He wasn't trying to sell himself to me. He was just letting me know what he'd advise as a coach. (As someone who works in advertising, I hate being sold anything. Give me the facts and I'll make up my own mind.)

Ironman is as much about getting to the start line uninjured as it is crossing the finishing line. You put a lot of strain on your body but it can cope surprisingly well if you build up the training properly.

We also talked about what type of races there are. Like I said, Ironman is now a huge global organisation. But there are also many long-distance events that aren't Ironman branded. So the choice was huge. Hot, cold, hilly, flat, in Europe, America, Asia, big, small etc.

Fran finished by saying that I didn't have to make a decision now. I should go and chat to my wife first. It takes up a lot of time and I'd need her support. Without it, it would be almost impossible.

I shook his hand and thanked him. I said I'd be in touch but I was pretty sure I'd made up my mind. Really, all I needed was for Julie to agree to me doing it. I knew she wouldn't actually say no but I had to at least discuss it with her and explain that I'd be either eating, training or sleeping for about the next ten months.

I went home and explained to Julie what Fran had said. She could see how excited I was by it. She actually thought it would be a good idea. She said if it's something you really want to do, then go for it. I said I'd try and do most of my training in the morning before work, then I'd have Saturday off and do my long bike ride on Sunday.

With Julie's support, there was nothing stopping me. I called Fran and said that I was up for it and I'd be interested in his help. All I had to do now was choose a race. I looked at loads on the internet. Some looked incredible. But realistically, I needed to do one in the UK.

In the back of my mind, I knew that my kidneys weren't getting any better. So if something went wrong, I didn't want to be hundreds of miles away from home. Ironman is an immense undertaking when you're well, never mind in my condition.

Finally, I decided on a race called the Outlaw in Nottingham, a 2.4-mile swim, a 112-mile bike ride, followed by a full marathon. I still couldn't imagine actually finishing this but with Fran's help I knew I'd be able to give it my best shot.

In between signing up for one of the toughest one-day endurance events in the world, I continued to visit the doctor's every six weeks.

I was now taking four different pills a day. My haemoglobin was slowly dropping and I'd begun to notice that occasionally my ankles got puffy as my body struggled to get rid of excess water.

One day, it was so bad that I went to my GP. When I explained what I was training for, he said in my condition it would not be physically possible. There was no way on earth I could complete the distances I talked about. He also said that there wasn't actually anything he could do to help the swelling. It was just part and parcel of kidney failure.

I was now beginning to see other symptoms, too. A month later, I had a painful attack of gout in my toe. It was agony. It's difficult to explain just how painful it is. It's constant pain. Even a duvet brushing against it caused pain. Putting trainers on was impossible. Normal paracetamol did nothing.

I struggled into work pretending it was no big deal. But I was in so much pain I could barely think straight. I lasted until lunchtime before having to go to a doctor down the road. They gave me some pills to get rid of it. She explained that it was caused by a build-up of uric acid because my kidneys weren't removing it properly and it was a common side-effect of kidney failure.

So apart from agonising attacks of gout, swollen ankles and lowering levels of haemoglobin, I was ready to start training for my big race.

My training would be broken into three rough areas. Base, build and peak. Base was slow, easy miles. Really, it was just getting my body into shape, ready for the training ahead. Build was where we started to increase the mileage, getting me ready for the longer, harder sessions ahead. Peak was where we started to lift the intensity. But this wouldn't be by much. There's little point smashing out a three-hour bike ride when, in reality, I'll be riding much slower for over six hours during the race.

I would also see Fran once a week for a strength session in the gym. Here, we'd work on specific stretches, making sure I didn't get injured. We also built up core strength, using free weights. This all sounds relatively easy. But when you've decided to hire an ex-military kickboxing marine who'd finished over seven Ironman races, this wasn't always the case.

On more than one occasion, I'd finish an intense circuit session by throwing up. Bizarrely, I quite enjoyed this (how I felt afterwards, not the actual throwing up), although I did question myself as to why I was actually paying someone to do this to me.

But before I started all this, I'd have to visit a podiatrist to check my running style. He could tell that I'd probably have trouble with my ITB (iliotibial band) because I had quite a lazy running style. However, he said he could hook up with Fran and make sure some of my strength exercises would be focused on my glutes. This should stop it being a problem as my mileage increased.

He also gave me a few pointers on running style. 'Don't run like a lazy fat girl.' This isn't really what he said but this was the gist of it.

Next, I had to get a proper bike fitting, on both my training bike and my new TT bike which I'd bought. For those who aren't into triathlon, TT is short for Time Trial. A time trial bike has two longer handle bars that attached to the front of the headset. It helps you get into a much more aerodynamic position.

This style of bike is favoured by most triathletes because all amateur races are non-drafting. You can't tuck behind another rider to use them as windbreak. This may not sound like much of big deal but riding behind another rider can make it up to 40 per cent easier. So riding in a tucked position can save you a lot of energy. When you're planning on cycling 112 miles followed by a marathon, this can only be a good thing.

I drove both my bikes to a shop in Putney. It was miles away from where I lived. But Fran knew the guy there and he was going to give me a discount. (Unsurprisingly, Julie had turned down the exciting offer of joining me.)

The guy who was going to measure me set up a bike on a frame so I could ride it and he could film me. First, I rode it as it was. Then he took pictures and huffed and puffed like a plumber sizing up a job before making a few adjustments. He then stuck small, round yellow stickers on various parts of my body and filmed again. I caught a glimpse of myself in the mirror covered in little yellow stickers. I looked a bit like Mister Blobby.

After a bit more filming and a few more adjustments, he said he'd finished. I should try riding in a low gear and then slowly increase it. It was incredible. Everything felt more fluid and being in the tuck position was much more comfortable. I was leaning on my elbows and I felt no pressure on my back at all. I was little sceptical at the start but I could now see it was worth it.

He then repeated the same procedure on my road bike. He gave me all the measurements and some before and after photos, so I could see how I was riding before and how I was riding now. The fitting was quite expensive but it would save a fortune in visits to a physio later. As I'd already discovered, trips to the physio usually hurt, so anything I could do to avoid this was a bonus.

I now had my running sorted and my bikes were a perfect fit. The next thing to sort out was my swimming.

Fran suggested that I call a guy he knew called Emile. He came highly recommended and lots of his other clients had used him. This was good enough for me. I gave him a call and arranged to meet him at the pool near where I worked. Emile had given them a call before we were due to meet and they said it would be fine for him to coach me there one morning.

The next day, I arrived to meet him. I'd got there early so I could warm up a bit first. I tried to swipe in using my card but as usual this didn't work. So the receptionist let me in without checking who I was. I could have used this place for years without paying and no one would have asked any questions.

I got into the changing room and the old guys who were always in there were getting changed. Two were incredibly posh. One was from the east end of London and the other was a Japanese guy. I loved listening to their conversations. They were like a comedy sketch. They spoke very slowly and clearly to the Japanese guy so he could understand them. The funny thing was, when he spoke, he spoke perfect English. He'd obviously been here for years. But they still spoke to him like he'd just arrived in England.

Another conversation I overheard was when one of them was telling the others that his grandson had come out as gay. He talked about it like it was some kind of disease. The older of the two posh guys said something along the lines of 'Oh, that's a real shame. Is there anyone he could go and see to, you know, get himself sorted out?' I couldn't believe what I was hearing. This was followed by the cockney bloke saying 'And he wanted to be an engineer... he won't be doing that now.' How would being gay stop you being an engineer?

Today, they were talking about *Strictly Come Dancing*. I won't go into details but it wasn't the men on the show they were talking about. For old guys they still, how can I put this, got very excited by the female form. I continued to eavesdrop on their conversation but stuck in a changing room surrounded by randy old men was not a place I wanted to stay, so I quickly finished getting changed and went off to the pool.

Emile soon turned up and we were chatting about how often I swam and what drills I did. There was a few I did, like one-armed swimming and doing lengths by just kicking but apart from building strength I had no idea how this actually helped.

He asked me to swim a few lengths and he'd watch me underwater to see where I was going wrong. The first thing he picked up on was that I 'windmilled' when I swum. My right arm was directly behind my left. It should be much smoother. I should hold the leading arm out in front for longer and almost let my other arm catch it up, before pulling the water behind me.

He showed me what he meant and I watched him swim. It looked effortless. There was no splashing. He just glided through the water like a dolphin. I must have looked like a hippo swimming compared to this.

Then I had a go. Surprisingly, just by changing my technique in this tiny way, it suddenly felt so much smoother. I still had a long way to go but I was amazed that, after about five minutes, I was a better swimmer. He gave me a load of drills to practice but warned me not to just do drills. If I did this, there was a danger I'd get great at doing drills and still be a bad swimmer.

He also noticed that I barely kicked my legs. They dragged behind me. Again, this would slow me down. He showed me how to kick properly. I tried to copy him but as I was still trying to remember what to with my arms, I ended up swallowing loads of water. After nearly drowning, I stopped by the side of the pool. He came over and said that

I should just concentrate on one drill at a time for now. I did a few more lengths concentrating on what he'd just showed me. It was far from perfect but he said with practice these few pointers should help me no end.

I was now finally ready to start training. I started quite slowly and the first month or so went without a hitch.

While I was planning all this, I was also in the middle of swapping jobs. The agency that we were in had huge financial difficulties. It had gone from being one of the best places in London to being a shadow of its former self. It's a shame because it had been great. But it was time leave.

When we resigned, we already had a new job to go. Two of our mates had put a word in for us and after what seemed like about 200 interviews, they offered us a job. It was a great place with loads of incredible clients. We (I was still working with Al) were over the moon.

We waited a few days and the contracts arrived. We signed them and posted them off. It was now official: we had a new job. All we had to do now was resign from our old place. Our old contracts stipulated that we had to work a three-month notice period but they let us go on what's called 'gardening leave'. All it really means is that you don't have to work your notice period but you still get paid.

I couldn't believe my luck. Three months off, fully paid. This was great. I was wondering how I'd fit in all my training, now I had plenty of time. Talk about perfect timing.

These few months flew by. The training was all base, so it was easy and slow. I had plenty of time to swim in the morning, have some lunch and a snooze, then go for a run in the afternoon. The following day, I'd be out on the bike then do some strength training. This was great. It was like being a professional, except they obviously train a lot harder and longer than I do.

It also saved me from three months of *Cash in the Attic* and *Jeremy Kyle*. For those not versed in daytime TV entertainment, the former is a programme in which a guy in a bad suit tries to flog off a load of old crap that he's found kicking around some old woman's home. The latter is where an annoying guy shouts at people in tracksuits with bad teeth. So I was glad to have the training to keep me occupied.

However, it was soon time to start my new job. This would make training more of a challenge. But it didn't take long to get used to getting up early and doing most of my training before the day even started. By the time I arrived at work I was wide-awake and ready to go, where most of the other people where still waking up.

To this day, I try and do as much of my training in the morning as possible. Plus, I'm very lucky that my offices are in Marylebone. There's a 30-metre pool about two minutes away. I can run around Hyde Park, Regent's Park and St James Park. Plus, there's about a four-mile loop around Regent's Park, which is great for cycling – and I had it all on my doorstep.

Another reason it was good to do it first thing is that you never know what's going to happen in work. A late meeting can really mess up your plans. So you have to do it afterwards, then you're home late. So get up, get it done, then you're free for the rest of the day, unless you're doing double sessions. If that's the case, do the long one in the morning and the shorter one after work.

I was now in a pretty good routine. Fran would send me all my sessions on Sunday night and I'd be set up for the week. Plus, I'd meet him once a week for the a gym session. We'd also talk about nutrition, recovery and what food I should eat during the race (and how much).

Fran could clearly see that this was a matter we needed to discuss after one particularly tough gym session. After about 35 minutes in, I started to feel dizzy. But for the next ten minutes or so, I pushed on. This was a big mistake. I can't remember what exercise I was doing but my vision started to go and I suddenly felt very sick. I staggered off to the toilet and threw up. I came back out looking as white as a sheet.

Fran suggested I take a break. While I rested, he chatted to me about what I'd eaten before I arrived. I'd had muesli for breakfast, and a cheese sandwich along with a packet of Mini Cheddars for lunch.

As I said this out loud, I was aware how ridiculous this sounded. It was little wonder I'd started to feel feint. It was no surprise to discover that I'd need something with a little more energy than two bits of bread and some cheese. From this moment onwards, I always made sure I had a decent meal. Just to be on the safe side, I always had a banana about 30 minutes before arriving.

Fran suggested I keep a food diary for a week, so he could see what I actually ate. I told him that, believe it or not, I had a pretty healthy diet. It was just today that, for some inexplicable reason, I'd chosen to eat a lunch that contained little or no nutrition.

He also encouraged me to do my long rides at the weekend on my own, too. It's the only way he could guarantee I trained at the right pace, although every now and then I'd join the club to keep myself sane.

On one of these occasions, one of the older guys who'd been there for years was leading out a large group of newbies on a novice ride. He told them how they should respect other road users. Always try to be courteous, give way to pedestrians and make sure that you remain calm at all times.

About two minutes into the ride, a van cut him up. He jumped off his bike and started shouting at the guy driving. The van driver gave him a load of abuse back and got out of the van. They were both now standing in the road, holding up the traffic, shouting at each other. One of the other guys joked to the rest of the novices that were watching, that this is what he meant by remaining calm.

For some reason, my kidneys didn't get any worse for these few months. My training was going well and part of my plan was to race a half-iron distance race near Barcelona (organised by Challenge) in a few weeks time. This would be a good place to see how my training was going before the full race in July. Things were shaping up nicely but then disaster struck.

I woke up at around 3am in agony. I recognised the searing pain in my foot instantly. It was another attack of gout, except this was much worse than last time. I tried to bend my toe and my whole body tensed up as I felt an electric bolt of pain shoot up my leg. I tried to get out of bed and but it took ages, it was so painful. I hobbled downstairs and took some paracetamol. This was a bit like using an egg cup of water to put out the fire of London. But it was all I had.

I stayed awake until the sun started to rise, trying to block out the pain. As soon as the doctor's opened, I gave them a call and got the first appointment available. Julie drove me to the doctor's and I hopped into reception. I was in agony. I could see that Julie was beginning to get really worried. It was beginning to become obvious that my kidney disease was really starting to affect me.

The only pain I've felt that matched this attack was when I'd had kidney stones as a teenager. To put this into perspective, most doctors will tell you that kidney stones are as painful, if not more so, than child birth.

I was in so much pain now, I was drenched in sweat. I couldn't take much more this. I started to get dizzy and then threw up. I collapsed into one the chairs in the waiting room, apologised to the staff as they helped me in to see the doctor. He recognised the symptoms straight away and gave me something that would get rid of it quite quickly.

He also gave me some much stronger painkillers. These would leave me in a happy fog for the rest of the day. As I sat there answering his questions, I realised I was supposed to be racing in Barcelona in seven days. I asked him if he thought I'd be OK. He said it was highly unlikely. While the pills he'd given me should work relatively quickly, swimming, cycling, then running half a marathon would be impossible as it would take a while for the joint to fully recover.

This was the first time my illness had affected my racing. Suddenly, it all seemed very real. Too real. I hated it. I limped off out of the surgery and headed into work. I tried to forget about it but the pain and sense of 'being ill' really got me down, although I tried not to show it. While I was training and racing, I felt well. Now I wasn't. For the first time, my illness was stopping me from doing what I loved and there was absolutely nothing I can do about it.

I was a gutted. I'd booked the flights, the accommodation, studied the course and there were a few other guys from the club going, too. It was all set to be a great race. Still, I'd paid for it all by now and I wouldn't be able to cancel it, so we went regardless. At the very least, I'd have few days off in the sun.

I still refused to believe 100 per cent that I couldn't race. So I packed up my bike and all my race stuff anyway. I knew there was only about a one per cent chance I'd make the start line. But one percent is better than zero per cent.

I'd booked a cheap EasyJet flight, which meant getting up at 3am to get to Gatwick for a 6am take-off. Because I had my bike with me in a bike box, I'd booked a people carrier to get us to the airport. The taxi driver turned up in a car that was little bigger than a Mini Metro. After a few minutes of faffing around, the cabbie informed me that the bike box wouldn't fit. He'd obviously just graduated from the school of 'pointing out the bleeding obvious'. He said he'd radio through to base and get another car sent out.

Half an hour later, a knackered old Peugeot turned up. The first car we couldn't fit in, the second looked like it would struggle to get us to the end of the road, let alone to the airport on time.

Instead of getting out to help us load the car, the driver just sat in the driver's seat. I don't expect to be waited on hand and foot but a little help would have been nice. If he wasn't going to give me hand, he could at least have helped Julie with her case, which, of course, weighed a ton.

After loading the car, we set off. Things didn't get much better from here on, either. When he found out we were going to Spain, he told us he thought going abroad was a waste of time. 'What's the point?' he said. 'The food's terrible. It's too hot and it costs a fortune.' Maybe he should ditch cab driving and take up writing for *Lonely Planet*.

He then went on to tell us about all the terrible flights he'd had. For someone who hated 'abroad', he'd done a lot of flying. Halfway through a particular story about bad turbulence over Turkey, it must have dawned on him that this wasn't the best topic of conversation for two customers he was driving to the airport. He then tried to reassure us by saying: 'Statistically, though, you're 98 per cent more likely to die in a car crash than you are in plane crash.' Looking at the state of the car we were in, I'd say it was 100 per cent more likely.

Eventually we arrived at the airport, alive, and boarded our plane, which according to driver was highly unlikely to crash. We landed safely and stepped out into the bright Spanish sunshine. In the back of my mind, I knew I was supposed to be racing here. So the fact it was beautifully sunny made the fact that I wasn't harder to bear.

The actual race venue was about an hour away from Barcelona on the coast, in a place called Calella. It wasn't the most picturesque place I've visited. It was heavily built up in the '70s as a tourist resort and it was beginning to show signs of wear and tear. We pulled up outside our hotel and all the other athletes were arriving, too.

Some had already checked in, others were checking their bikes, a few of them were out running. This may sound like a crazy thing to do a couple of days before a big race but as long as you don't push yourself, it will help. After months of training, slowly building up to the event, the second you stop your body will go into repair mode. So if you just stop dead a few days before a race, you can wake up on race day feeling tired and sluggish.

We checked into our room and went out to explore. I was still limping a little but even now, with two days until the race, I thought there might be a slim chance I'd be OK. So as we wandered around, I kept my eyes peeled for somewhere that did pasta. Somewhere I could have a pre-race meal.

If I'd wanted a full English breakfast or a roast dinner, I'd have been fine. This entire resort clearly catered for a certain type of British tourist. Some of the adverts outside the restaurants proudly claimed that they served 'BRITISH SAUSAGES!' and 'BISTO'. This was the exact opposite of what I ate on holiday. I liked to try all the local stuff. Most of what was on offer here could be found in any old UK high street.

Eventually, we found somewhere. It had a range of Tapas, along with a few simple pasta dishes. This would be perfect. As we wandered through the back alleys, we could hear the faint sound of music coming from the Expo. This is a place where all the athletes gather to buy last-minute bits and pieces and admire all the equipment that's on offer.

I hobbled round looking at all kinds of stuff. As I stood back admiring a bike which cost more than a small house, I bumped into Rob, Arvid and Ed, the guys from the club. I told them that due to an injury I wouldn't be racing but I'd come and watch them. I found out what waves they were in and left them to stock up on water bottles, gels and all the other stuff they'd undoubtedly buy.

The next day, I woke up and I could actually walk without limping. I tried to run and it was just about possible. I was still convinced that racing was an option. However, after about 30 seconds, it became clear that my one per cent chance had become zero per cent. I could probably swim and finish the bike but hobbling around a half-marathon would be a daft idea. I could damage myself permanently.

Julie and I spent most of the rest of the day sunbathing. While all the other athletes rushed around, getting ready, I sat back and enjoyed the sun. After a Serrano Ham Bocadillo and a cold beer, things didn't look so bad. I still had my main goal, so all was not lost.

On the Sunday I watched Rob, Arvid and Ed race. I sat outside the hotel and watched the bike section. Some these guys were really hammering it. After the cyclists thinned out, I went to the finish to watch the runners. It was a brutally hot day and I was burning up just standing in the sun, so running in it would have been really tough.

I saw Rob finish first. If I remember rightly, he finished in around four hours, 20 minutes. Ed came in next. I think he was just under five hours. I've forgotten what time Arvid did it in but in these conditions whatever you time was, it was still a mighty achievement.

Seeing as I'd brought my bike, I thought it was daft not use it. So I put it together and headed out on to the bike course. All the others had long since finished but I could at least get a glimpse of what I was missing. The cycle route was incredible. A long, fast, flat winding road that hugged the coastline. It would have been great. But rather than dwell on what I'd missed, I tried to focus on what was coming up.

After a couple of hours out on the bike I returned to the room to get showered, so Julie and I could enjoy our last night. As we wandered around deciding what we should eat, we bumped into the others.

I offered to buy them all a beer as a way of congratulating them. So we all had a couple of bottles of Estrella before going our separate ways.

That night, Julie and I went out and had the best meal of our entire trip. I had fresh fish, caught that day, and chips. They had a small barbecue out the back, where they grilled the fish, and it was delicious. It was a nice end to what had started off as a bit of a doomed trip.

The following day, we were back up early to fly home. I managed to load all my stuff back into the hire car and we left with plenty of time. It was just as well because the the road we needed to take to get back to the airport was closed.

We tried to follow the diversion signs but we just ended up getting more and more lost.

Starting to panic, I searched the car for a map. Luckily, I found one in the back of the car. Once we'd actually worked out where we were, Julie guided me back to the airport. Having had to get up incredibly early, I was glad to get on the plane and go to sleep. We arrived back at Gatwick to the usual cold, damp welcome.

All we needed to do was find our taxi driver. He wasn't hard to spot. He was outside Costa Coffee holding a sign which read 'Dillion Dover'. Since my first day at school, everyone I've met has struggled with my name. Dinken Doover. Dollan Driver and my personal favourite Chicken Diver. I'd heard and seen them all.

Unlike the last driver, at least he offered to help Julie with her case, although the second he took it off her he probably wished he hadn't been so helpful. I struggled behind them with a bike box that now had a wheel missing, courtesy of Gatwick's delicate baggage handlers. We followed him out of the airport and into the car park right up to his car, a tiny little hatchback which looked like it would be suitable for a family of pygmies.

I sighed, deleted the cab company's number from my phone and waited as he called the office to send out a bigger car.

Re-Focus

I WAS disappointed to miss the race in Barcelona but I soon picked myself up. At least it hadn't happened the week before my main race.

After a week or so, my gout had passed and I was back up to full training. Apart from the fact I was like a water balloon full of uric acid (the acid that causes gout), I also had a suspicion that I wasn't drinking enough when I trained. So I started weighing myself before and after each ride or run to make sure I wasn't over or under-hydrating, although on one occasion my over-hydrating caused me to be chased by an angry farmer.

I stopped at the top of a hill, by a fence, opposite a cottage, and looked around to make sure the coast was clearer. I was busting for a pee and couldn't see any harm in going there. As I relaxed and felt the kind of relief that you only get from going to the toilet when you've been holding it in for ages, I heard a voice – and it wasn't friendly.

A farmer was running towards me shouting at me. I couldn't stop mid-flow, so I just tried to go harder. But it just kept on coming. I could have filled a reservoir. But as I continued to go, the farmer got closer. I finished as quickly as I could, tucked myself in, jumped on my bike and cycled off down the hill. The farmer shouted after me – but I was long gone.

At the bottom of the hill, I noticed there was a small peloton of cyclists turning right. I caught up with them and followed them. It must have been a local sportive. I should have been doing a long, slow, aerobic ride. But I was soon caught up in the sportive. About an hour later, I remembered that I was supposed to be doing an easy ride. Oops. I turned off and headed home. Despite my little detour, I was feeling OK. Not great but OK. But this was the last time I remember feeling like this. From here on in, every training session was a struggle.

As I continued to train, I could feel myself getting worse, more tired and slower. In theory, with around nine weeks to go, I should be close to hitting my peak. But I had reached my plateau and was finding it harder and harder.

I can still remember my final long run into work. I woke up at 5.30am and dragged myself out of bed. It was cloudy and dark, and as I set off it started to rain. Not heavily, just drizzle, enough for me to get wet. I slowly shuffled on. I was exhausted. My low levels of haemoglobin were now really starting to effect me. How on earth could I run a marathon after a 180km bike ride if I couldn't make a simple run into work?

Again, something inside me spurred me on. I refused to give up. Why? I've no idea. I guess you're either born with this kind of mindset or you're not. Or maybe the doctor was right and there really was something wrong with my brain.

Around two hours in, the negative thoughts started to take over. I wanted to just give up and go home as the doubts started to play out in my head. What's the point? Who am I kidding? This is crazy. You're ill and there's nothing you can do about it. What are you trying to prove anyway? Just give up. Just. Give. Up.

I'd read about the psychological fight that long-distance athletes often have with themselves and this was my first taste of it. You had to suck it up. Work through the dark patch, because you will feel better. This is just part of what you have to go through. I reassured myself that if it was easy, anyone could do it.

Negative thoughts can also be a sign that you need some food. So I finished the banana I had with me, had a gel and stopped at a shop to get some water before carrying on.

I slowly started to feel better. I was going to finish my last long run. I actually started to speed up. I made it into work, soaked and knackered, but I'd made it. I still had no idea how I'd actually finish the race but I'd won this psychological battle. Willpower 1 negative thoughts 0. Once again, I'd proven to myself that if you set your mind to something, nothing can stop you.

After this session, I had one more long week of training before it was time to taper. It looked something like this:

Monday Meet Fran for gym session

Tuesday Swim 1km am/Bike 1hr easy (last 20 mins high cadence) pm

Wednesday Bike 1hr easy + 10k brick (faster than race pace)

Thursday Swim 600m warm-up/600m pull only /10x200m @ race pace/400m cool down

Friday Interval run 5x1km @ 4min 30 (1min easy in-between)

Saturday Rest

Sunday Bike 6hrs

I also had one last doctor's appointment a few weeks before the race and then I'd get to see if, after ten months training, I could complete the longest race of my life.

My kidney function had now dropped to 25 per cent. The doctor told me that I would now need to be transferred to Guy's Hospital renal department, where they would look after me. He explained that they would monitor me until they thought I'd need a transplant or start dialysis. It was strange to be saying goodbye to him. I'd been seeing him for so long, I'd actually got to know him quite well.

He shook my hand, wished me well and said that he was sure I'd be fine. He didn't say anything about the race. I think he must have assumed I'd given up on that idea.

Going Long

JULIE met me after work and we headed off to Nottingham. I was so tired on the way up that we had to stop at a service station so I could have a sleep. I don't know what my level my haemoglobin was at now but I now felt tired all of the time. It crossed mind that if I was struggling to drive from London to Nottingham, swimming, cycling and running the equivalent distance would surely be impossible.

We arrived in Nottingham to meet my mum and dad, who'd come along to support me. My brother and his wife, Megan, were going to arrive on race day, which was Sunday.

That night we all went for an Italian, so I could carb-load. i.e. eat too much pasta. I'm glad I wasn't racing on Saturday as I think I overdid it a bit. Now I knew how Pavarotti felt. I ate so much pasta and bread, I felt like I might explode.

We had a quick drink in the bar and then I got an early night. The next day, I had an enormous amount of fannying about to do. I'd have to sort my bike out, check all my kit then check it again. I was bound to have left something behind, so this would mean a mad dash to a bike shop just before it closed.

I'd also have to go to the race briefing, rack my bike, pick up my transition bags, hang them up etc etc, but now I just needed to sleep because on race day I'd have to get up at 3.30am.

I woke up around 9am on Saturday and me and Julie went down for breakfast. It was clear who else was racing. You can spot triathletes anywhere in the world. If the finishers' T-shirt doesn't give them away, their trainers will. If their trainers don't, their shaved legs will. If their sunglasses don't give them away, their sun visors will. It's like a pre-race uniform. No one has to wear it but pretty much all of them do.

I was going to have a healthy breakfast, but couldn't resist scrambled eggs on toast, with baked beans, some bacon and a wafer-thin slither of black pudding

After the breakfast of champions, I drove to the venue to drop off my stuff and attend the race briefing. There were a lot of fit seriously fit athletes there. There was less body fat here than at a catwalk show at London Fashion Week.

Most of the people I knew had already commented that I looked ill (well I was) because I weighed about 11 stone. But a lot of the athletes here were just muscle, bone and skin. They were as aerodynamic as their bikes.

This did little to settle my nerves. Then I saw a chubby bloke and thought 'well at least I won't come last'. I also thought 'good on him'. He wasn't sitting around moaning about his 'glands'. He was about to take part in one of the toughest amateur races you could enter. If I'd worn a hat, I'd have taken it off to him.

The announcer called all the athletes (I like to include myself in this term but who am I kidding?) to the race briefing. This was pretty straightforward and it covered all the usual points. I'd heard all this before.

Just as I thought this, the announcer said: 'I'm not worried about the athletes who are doing this as their first race, they'll listen to everything I'll have to say. It's the athletes who think they've heard it all before, they're the ones that usually come unstuck.' So I listened intently for the rest of the briefing.

We were then free to go. Go eat, go rest and go to sleep. Ready for the race of our lives.

3.30am.

My alarm went off and woke me with a start. I'd slept quite well. I quietly got dressed and went down to have some breakfast. I thought it would only be the people racing who were up but there were a couple of stag dos and hen dos that hadn't been to bed yet.

So I ended up sharing my early breakfast with a load of drunk people, including a very drunk guy called Davo. I know his name because every time he downed another Tequila, all his mates chanted 'Davo! Davo!' until he had to run outside and be sick. True to form, at least two of the girls from the hen do were crying. This was a very odd start to the day.

I finished my breakfast and drove to the venue. I'd told Julie and my mum and dad not to bother coming until the start of the run. There wouldn't be much to see on the swim. On the bike, they'd see me for about five seconds. Bedsides, if I made it that far, I'd need all the help I could get on the run.

At the venue, I put on my wetsuit ready for the off. We were called to get into the water. I got in and...f...f...f... it was freezing. Everyone else seemed fine but this hurt it was so cold. Then I realised what it was.

My haemoglobin was so low that I felt cold most of the time anyway. So getting in a cold lake was hell. I was shivering, I was so cold. My teeth had started chattering. I was beginning to wonder if I'd last the swim, never mind the rest of it. If we could just get started, I'd be OK.

The announcer counted down from five, four, three, two, one and, bang, I was off.

Focus and breathe. Try and find some space. Kick. Punch. Gulp. Breathe.

God it's cold. Splash. Sight. Swim. Remember to kick. Come on, you can do this. Get out of my way. Ouch. Remember, technique. Long, slow strokes. Long slow strokes and breathe. Sight. Stroke. Breathe. God it's cold. Must keep sighting.

Follow the guy in front. Make it easy for yourself. What's that sign? 400m? No, 200m. So, 3,800m minus 200m, that's

3,600m to go. Just keep pushing. Need a wee. Mmmm, nice and warm. Must be a good sign. You've hydrated well. Look up. There are a lot of people in front. Look back. And some behind. What's that sign? 1,000m, getting there slowly. Just keep going. The sun's coming up.

Getting warmer. Can't see. Keep going. Is that the turn? Yes! Halfway there. Just the same again. Turn, swim back to the start. Going to make it. Get off my feet. Swim faster. No, calm down. Focus. Slow and steady. Starting to get cold again. Really cold. This hurts. Speed up to warm up. Speed up to warm up. Speed up to warm up. Sight. Slow and steady. Hands starting to cramp. This is so cold. I can hear music. Nearly there. Get blood back into legs. Kick. Kick. Kick. Can hear the music. Up the bank.

So, so cold. Come on hands, work. Cramp. Cramp. Cramp. Yes, I need help. So cold. Thanks. Right, concentrate. Into transition tent. What's my number? 1521. Find my bag. Find somewhere to sit. Glad I packed arm warmers. Bike shoes on. Thank God that's over. Find bike. Where did I leave it? By the pole. There are poles everywhere. Right, there she is. Let's go. Nice easy spin to get going. Sun's out, nice day. Nice day for racing. And finishing.

Blimey, I'm flying. Eat! Drink! Keep focused. Must remember food. Keep the pedals turning. This is great. Camera, don't smile, try and look cool. Keep eating. 'The bike should be like a rolling buffet.' Wise words. That's a lot of supporters. Keep pushing. Right, I'll race you. No, focus. Race your own race. No one else's. Where's the hill. I thought there was a hill at 30 miles. Oh here it is, shit. This is hard. Nothing, no energy.

Slow easy spin. Getting slower. This hill isn't even that big. Lungs burning, legs hurting. Come on, push, focus. Just look a couple of metres ahead. Spin spin spin. Top coming near. Eat, drink, eat, drink. Aid station. Take on new bottles. Drop off old. Eat. Halfway point coming up. Blimey, that's quick, too quick. I could go under 12. Not bad. That would be great.

Calculate marathon time on bike so far plus half... brain not working. Eat, drink. I could go under 12. In Ironman, the real race starts with the run. Stay confident. But don't get ahead of yourself. Why have I got a Smiths song going round my head? Some girl's mothers are bigger than other girl's mothers... aid station, more drink, more food. Gels, time to move on to gels, remember what you practiced. Some girl's mothers are bigger than other girl's mothers. 40km to go. Blimey, that was quick.

Oh dear, have I over cooked it? Feel much better than I thought. More drink, another gel, need to go to the toilet. Wait until transition, wait until... got to go. Stop by this bush. Back hurts, quick stretch, arghhh, that feels good. Some girl's mothers are bigger than others girl's mothers... get back on the bike. Get spinning, easy. Easy. Pick up speed now. Just keep pushing to the end. Overtake. Don't get caught drafting. Move over. Keep going. Eat. Drink. 20km to go now.

Whatever happens, I can finish now. Even if I have to walk the marathon. I'm going to do this. I'm only going to go and finish this. 5km to go. Easy gear, get the legs ready. Spin, spin, spin. Transition! At last. Not many other bikes here. Blimey, that was quick. Rack bike, take a gel. Look, I can see them. Mum, dad, Julie, Mark and Megan. Get a boost, smile, wave, hide the pain. Shit, this is going to hurt. Really hurt. My back is killing me. Small steps, just don't slow down. Sun coming out. Heating up. Slowing down. Energy gel.

Pain increasing. Shuffle. Shuffle. Getting hot. Just to the next aid station. Drink. Food. pretzels? Oh yeah, for salt. Just to the next aid station. Slower. Hotter. Harder. Just to the next aid station. Lap one done. That was very slow. Three to go. Getting overtaken now. Overtaken a lot. Hands puffing up. Oh no, this is not a good sign. Sausages. Sausages. I sound like that talking dog. Keep drinking. But have I drunk too much?

Are my kidneys failing now? Shit. Oh god. Need to find a medic. Just. To. The. Next. Aid. Station. Drink. Eat. Medic. I've got kidney disease. Need pulse check. Yes, only

20 per cent function. No idea how I've got this far. Good to continue? Great. I'll take it easy. Yes, I'll stop by and see you in the medical tent at end. Just 10km to go. Can't run now. Just keep shuffling.

This is really slow. Don't care. Going to finish. Going to finish. Must finish. There's mum and Julie, dad, Mark and Megan. Heat. Pain. Suffering. Finishing my last lap. Take a photo. Can't stop. Won't ever start again. Finally. One kilometre to go.

Thirteen hours and five minutes. Jog the last bit. *Diccon Driver, you are an Outlaw!* Stagger over the line. Hold up finish tape. Smile? Grimace. You've done it. You've done it. Into medical tent. Blimey, it looks like a war zone. Blood pressure check. Good to go? Great. Food. God, I'm hungry. Eat, eat, eat, find Julie. Big sweaty hug. Mum and dad. Sweaty hug. All finished.

All finished. Made it alive. Rehydrate. Eat. Rehydrate, eat. Sit. Down. Rest. Rest. Rest. Feel exhausted, elated. Tired, excited. That's some achievement. In my condition. In your condition? Hot. Tired. Hungry. Thirteen hours, 16 minutes. Ten months training.

Finished.

Finished.

Finished.

I hobbled around with all the other athletes picking up their stuff. This must be what it's like to have arthritis. We all slowly made our way back to our cars. It looked a bit like a scene from the walking dead.

One guy was having to carry his two-year-old on his shoulders. The little guy was jumping up and down, causing his dad all kinds of pain. But he soldiered on. At least all I had to carry was my transition bags.

We drove back to the hotel and headed to the multi-storey car park. I tried to park as close as I could to the hotel. Of course, we ended up on the top floor before I could find a space.

I shuffled into the bar ordered a pint of coke, a burger and chips. But strangely, I wasn't that hungry now. A day of gels hadn't done my stomach much good and the wind I was producing would have violated the Geneva Convention's law on the use of chemical weapons. If I released much more of this, I'd be classed as a biohazard. It was eye wateringly bad.

I ate half the burger, had a few chips, a protein shake and staggered off upstairs, leaving behind me a cloud of green fog. My mum hugged me and said congratulations. Then my dad gave me a big hug and he told me that he was really proud of me. Just for second, I felt like a small boy again who had done well at sports day. I don't think it matters how old you are, there's a part of you that will always want to make your parents proud of you.

Back in the room, I called Fran. He sounded relieved to hear from me and that I'd finished alive and in one piece. (Dead athletes don't look good on the CV.) He congratulated me and said what I'd achieved was incredible. All I had to do now was rest and relax.

I didn't need telling twice. I spent most of the night lolling around on the bed, slowly getting hungry. I slept like a baby. (Since writing this and having a baby, I know how ridiculous this saying is. 'Slept like a baby' would literally mean being awake all night, needing my nappy changed two or more times and constantly needing to be fed.) But for the sake of this story, let's assume it meant that I slept solidly for ten hours before getting up and eating the mother of all breakfasts.

Driving home, I was exhausted. Post-race and low haemoglobin levels made it incredibly difficult to keep my eyes open. Unlike last time, I decided to swerve the Red Bull. Still knackered, I got home and lay around on the sofa while Julie looked after me. It still seemed odd that I'd finished.

I woke up the next day and the enormous sense of achievement hadn't passed. What did feel odd was that it was all over. I now had no goal. (Obviously I had things I wanted to achieve at work but nothing of the sporting nature). From the first Olympic distance race I'd done, I'd been building to this in one way or another for over six years.

I'd gone from thinking it was impossible – even the doctor had told me that – to actually swimming 2.4 miles, cycling 112 miles and running a full marathon with a haemoglobin level that's half the average and only 20 per cent kidney function. Without trying to sound like one of those motivational memes you see on Facebook, if you put your mind to it, you really can accomplish anything. The only barrier is you.

The more I race, and the more I learn about the human body, the more amazed I am by what it can do. And it all stems from a positive mindset. And not being afraid to fail.

So it was with this kind of mindset that I decided to take on my new challenge – kidney failure. It was now no longer if but when they'd fail. And I'd have to face up to my biggest fears. As with all fears, the biggest normally stems from the unknown.

Would my brother be a match? Could I put him through this? If we went through with the transplant, would I have to go on dialysis first, while I waited for the tests. Even if the operation went ahead, would my body accept it? Would my brother be able to live a normal life afterwards?

I'd eventually find out all the answers to these questions and more, starting with another check-up and my first meeting with a renal transplant nurse.

This Is It

I ARRIVED at Guy's Hospital and went up to the renal clinic. I had a meeting with a nurse called Jude.

She started by telling me that the fact I'd had an offer from a family member to be a donor was great. She also told me that it takes, on average, six months for the donor to be 'worked up' ready for the operation.

Judging by my current results, it was highly likely that I'd have to go on dialysis.

But before we made any kind of plan, they wanted more blood. I had to do another urine test. As I waited for the results, I listened to the other patients' conversations. Some had just discovered they had kidney disease, others had had the operation and some were already on dialysis.

One guy was recovering from a recent transplant. His new kidney was working but not very well and the hospital were doing everything they could to kick-start it. In my mind, I had an image of someone starting an old petrol lawn mower, repeatedly pulling the starting cord until it spluttered into life.

Another guy was on the phone to his wife or girlfriend. He'd only just found out he had kidney disease but it was quite advanced and he'd have to start dialysis in a few months. He was telling her he'd be fine. But as he spoke to her, I could hear his voice beginning to crack as his brave facade began to slip. He was quite a big guy. He looked like a builder or a scaffolder, someone who did a quite tough physical job. But when it comes to facing your own mortality, I defy anyone not to show their true emotions.

His voice quivered, and broke. He couldn't hold it back any longer. His eyes welled up with tears, which he wiped away with his shovel-like hands. The poor guy was terrified of what was going to happen to him. Like we all were. But at least my shock wasn't out of the blue. I'd had years to mentally prepare myself.

The girl sat to the left of me had recently had a transplant and I gathered that the donor was her sister. The two girls messed about together, laughing and joking. She said that she couldn't believe how much better she felt. I was considering interrupting their conversation to tell her sister how amazing she was for saving her sick sibling's life. But I'm sure she'd heard it from her already. Besides, I knew we were in a hospital but we were still in London, where there's an unwritten rule that you don't talk to strangers. If a stranger tried to talk to you they were probably mad and the correct course of action would be to ignore them completely, while planning your escape route.

As every form of human emotion played out around me, a softly spoken Australian nurse came over to me and asked if I was Diccon Driver, here to see Jude? She said 'hello, I'm Jude, would like to come into my office?' I nodded and followed, too scared to talk. We both sat down and I prepared myself for the news I'd been dreading. I could feel my stomach muscles physically tense as I prepared myself for a medical punch in the guts.

'I'm afraid it's not good news,' Jude said.

'Your GFR is now 18. You have just 18 percent kidney function and your haemoglobin is now eight. So it's highly likely in a month or two you'll have to go on dialysis.'

The word 'dialysis' hung in the silence of the room, just the low rumble of the air conditioning keeping it from being completely quiet.

I protested that I felt OK. But deep down, I knew I was anything but.

Looking back now, I realise I was scared. I was just trying to put off the inevitable. I told her about the race, and the distances, like it might make a difference to her prognosis. For a moment, she was left speechless. She asked me the distances again, as if she'd misheard me. I could see her mental calculating how far this actually was.

She said she had patients at the same stage as me who get out of breath walking up flights of stairs. Racing for 13 hours would… how an earth? Her voice trailed off because she could see I was upset. She then just looked at me, not saying a word. It's like she could actually see the news slowly sinking in.

She put a comforting hand on my arm and gently reassured me that I'd be fine. Apart from my kidneys, I was fit and healthy. Most importantly, I had an offer from a donor. I tried to look on the bright side. But even with my optimistic view, it was hard.

Really hard.

She said I should come back next week for a couple of scans and various other tests, so they could get me ready for dialysis. She gave me a bundle of leaflets and a DVD that showed me the various options. I thanked her, picked up my bundle of goodies and headed off back to work.

I arrived at work to find out something we'd been working on had been blown out. Everyone was panicking. I found it hard to share their urgency but I was actually glad of the distraction. For the next few hours, I just picked up where I'd left off. I was just another creative in an ad agency trying to get good work made.

It wasn't until I left work a few hours later that I started to dwell on the news that Jude had given me. I felt like I was in a bubble, moving in slow motion. As everyone else got on with their business without a care in the world, I boarded the train and gazed out of the window watching the lights of Canary Wharf slowly vanish in the distance, deep in thought. I was so deep in thought that I nearly missed my stop. But just in time I realised and pushed my way out on to the platform.

That night, I looked at the information Jude had given me. I've tried a few ways to describe the different types of dialysis. But the best example and the easiest to understand can be found on the NHS website. This is roughly what it says:

Haemodialysis:
Before haemodialysis can start, you'll usually need to have a special blood vessel created in your arm, called an AV fistula. This blood vessel is created by connecting an artery to a vein. Joining the two together makes the blood vessel larger and stronger. This makes it easier to transfer your blood into the dialysis machine and back again.

The operation to create the AV fistula is usually carried out around four to eight weeks before haemodialysis begins. This allows the tissue and skin surrounding the fistula to heal.

As a short-term measure, or in an emergency, you may be given a neck line. This is where a small tube is inserted into a vein in your neck.

The haemodialysis process:
Most people need three sessions of haemodialysis a week, with each session lasting around four hours. This can be done in hospital, or at home if you've been trained to do it yourself.

Two thin needles will be inserted into your AV fistula and taped into place. One needle will slowly remove blood and transfer it to the dialysis machine. The dialysis machine is made up of a series of membranes that act as filters and a special liquid called dialysate.

The membranes filter waste products from your blood, which are passed into the dialysate fluid. The used dialysate fluid is pumped out of the dialyser and the filtered blood is passed back into your body through the second needle.

During your dialysis sessions, you will sit or lie on a couch, recliner or bed.

If you're having haemodialysis, the amount of fluid you can drink will be severely restricted.

This is because the dialysis machine won't be able to remove two to three days' worth of excess fluid from your blood in just four hours. This can lead to serious problems where excess fluid builds up in your blood, tissues and lungs.

The amount of fluid you're allowed to drink will depend on your size and weight. Most people are only allowed to drink 1,000-1,500ml (two to three pints) of fluid a day.

You'll also need to be careful what you eat while having haemodialysis because minerals such as sodium (salt), potassium and phosphorus that would normally be filtered out by your kidneys can build up to dangerous levels quickly between treatment sessions.

The other option was peritoneal dialysis. This is how it explained that process:

There are two main types of peritoneal dialysis:
- *Continuous ambulatory peritoneal dialysis (CAPD) – where your blood is filtered several times during the day*
- *Automated peritoneal dialysis (APD) – where a machine helps filter your blood during the night as you sleep*

Both treatments can be done at home once you've been trained to carry them out yourself. They're described in more detail below.

Before you can have CAPD or APD, an opening will need to be made in your abdomen. This will allow the dialysis fluid to be pumped into the space inside your abdomen (the peritoneal cavity).

An incision is usually made just below your belly button. A thin tube called a catheter is inserted into the incision and the opening will normally be left to heal for a few weeks before treatment starts.

The catheter is permanently attached to your abdomen, which some people find difficult. If you're unable to get used to the catheter, you can have it removed and switch to haemodialysis instead.

Another option is continuous ambulatory peritoneal dialysis (CAPD)

The equipment used to carry out this process is:
- *A bag containing dialysate fluid*
- *An empty bag used to collect waste products*
- *A series of tubing and clips used to secure both bags to the catheter*
- *A wheeled stand that you can hang the bags from*

At first, the bag containing dialysate fluid is attached to the catheter in your abdomen. This allows the fluid to flow into the peritoneal cavity, where it's left for a few hours.

While the dialysate fluid is in the peritoneal cavity, waste products and excess fluid in the blood passing through the lining of the cavity are drawn out of the blood and into the fluid.

A few hours later, the old fluid is drained into the waste bag. New fluid from a fresh bag is then passed into your peritoneal cavity to replace it, and left there until the next session. This process of exchanging the fluids is painless and usually takes about 30-40 minutes to complete.

Exchanging the fluids isn't painful, but you may find the sensation of filling your abdomen with fluid uncomfortable or strange at first. This should start to become less noticeable as you get used to it.

Most people who use CAPD need to repeat this around four times a day. Between treatment sessions, the bags are disconnected and the end of the catheter is sealed.

Finally, there was Automated peritoneal dialysis (APD for short)

Automated peritoneal dialysis (APD) is similar to CAPD, except a machine is used to control the exchange of fluid while you sleep.

You attach a bag filled with dialysate fluid to the APD machine before you go to bed. As you sleep, the machine automatically performs a number of fluid exchanges. You'll usually need to be attached to the APD machine for 8-10 hours. At the end of the treatment session, some dialysate fluid will be left in your abdomen. This will be drained during your next session.

Despite the fact that APD would involve the area behind my stomach being filled with around a litre of liquid for most of the day, this sounded like the best option. It also meant that I could continue to exercise. I'd just have to manually drain out the fluid, do whatever I wanted, then drain another litre bag back in again.

The next week, I was in and out of hospital every five minutes. They scanned my heart, checked my veins, weighed me, tested my urine and took enough blood to keep a family of hungry vampires happy for the foreseeable future.

Jude, my renal nurse, also told me that my haemoglobin was now so that I really needed to start EPO injections. Being into cycling, I was well aware of what EPO was. It was one of the drugs favoured by cyclists in the dark days of the Tour de France. The reason it was so popular with endurance athletes was because it boosts red blood cell production, the cells that help carry oxygen around the body.

I asked Jude how often I'd have to come in and have these injections. She smiled and said: 'You don't have to come in. You just "needle" yourself.'

This sounded horrible but when she showed me the size of the needle, it looked pretty easy.

We practiced a few times on a pillow. Then it was my turn to do it on myself. The needle was tiny. But it's a really odd feeling to actually stick a needle in yourself. It stung a bit but it wasn't painful at all really.

I used to get weekly deliveries of these needles to work. I'd sneak off to the toilet, give myself the injection then go back to my desk. If anyone had accidently walked in, it would have looked like a scene from *Trainspotting*, I'd have trouble explaining that away.

I was also told that, along with EPO, I'd need iron infusions. This should help me feel a bit less wiped out all the time. It should also stop me feeling freezing cold. Even on a hot day, I'd wear a T-shirt, a long sleeved thermal top, with a normal shirt over the top of it. I started to think I'd be spending my life in hospital, able to pop into work on Tuesday between the hours of 2pm and 3.30pm.

Two weeks later, I was ready to go in and have the operation to get the tube put into my stomach. I arrived at the Richard Bright Ward at Guy's Hospital at around 9am. The plan was to operate at around 11am. I'm not sure why I had to be there so early but by now I felt so shit most of the time that I actually wanted to start dialysis. Plus, Jude had told me that at my stage it would actually make me feel a bit better.

After an hour of waiting outside the reception, I was finally given a bed. They fitted a cannula to my hand and told me that someone would be with me in a sec. Well, seconds turned to minutes, minutes turned to hours and, at around 3pm, they said they were nearly ready for me. I was beginning to think that it wasn't kidney disease that would kill me. I'd die of boredom long before that.

Then, all hell broke lose. Someone was rushed into the bed opposite me. I couldn't see whether it was a man or woman and before I got a chance to be nosey, the curtains were closed around them. Loads of doctors, nurses and all the other people who populate hospitals kept popping in and out.

It turned out the person who had just arrived had been waiting for a kidney for a few years. They were at work when they got call from a hospital saying a kidney had suddenly become available and they should get to hospital as soon as they could.

This meant I would have to wait until tomorrow. But I couldn't really moan. The average wait for a kidney for someone who doesn't have the option of a transplant stands at around two to three years. If you have a rare blood group or are from an ethnic background, it could be up to five. This is because of the simple reason there are not enough people who have registered to be donors. So if you're reading this and haven't already registered, please sign up today.

The next morning, I was woken at 6am. The surgeon was ready. I'd spoken to the anaesthetist and I was ready to go. I lay on the operating table and a mask was put over my face. I was told to take a deep breath and count backwards from ten, nine, eight, seven, six…

Before I knew it, I was sitting back in the ward grinning like an idiot, while the drugs they'd used to knock me out wore off.

Julie had come to visit me and thankfully she'd brought food. During this entire process, up to including the present day, I can't fault the NHS' medical skill. The food, however, left a lot to be desired. It also left a lot to your imagination. Most of it was so bad that you could only guess what it was.

The next morning, I was woken at 5.30am to have my blood pressure and temperature taken. It was OK, so the nurse told me I could go home. She gave me a prescription for more pills, which I could pick from the pharmacy on the way out. This took forever but I didn't care because I was going home and I would be able to get some sleep.

I went outside and the weather matched how I was feeling – grey, foggy and pretty miserable. Thankfully, one of my mates, Andy, had taken the day off work to drive me home. This meant I wouldn't have to bother with the train, which I really didn't fancy because the front of my abdominal area was still pretty sore from the operation.

I now had a week off to sit around and recover. I was told under no circumstances to lift anything heavy. The next day, all the fluid for the dialysis machine turned up. Twenty-four boxes loaded with fluid bags arrived at my front door. Needless to say, they weighed a ton.

I slowly took all the boxes upstairs and put them in the spare room. Each night, I'd have to load one of these bags on the dialysis machine before plugging myself in.

After being trained back at the hospital on how to put the machine together, I started dialysing through the night. It took a while to get used to. But after a week, I was back at work and most people had little or no idea what I was going through. They knew I was ill but that was about it. That's the way I liked it. It meant I could get on with my job and try and keep things as normal as possible.

I slowly started cycling again too, just into work and back but this added up to about 25 miles a day. It took me about 20 minutes longer than before but I was determined to keep it up.

Slowly, things got (relatively) back to normal. I say 'relatively' because there was a list of things I could and couldn't do now I started peritoneal dialysis.

I couldn't get the exit site for the tube that was ticking out of my side wet (this meant no swimming) in case it got infected. If it got infected, I'd have to have it removed.

If I had a shower, I had to make sure it was completely covered.

I had to clean the exit point of the tube every morning and every evening.

I couldn't drink too much fluid because my body couldn't get rid of it.

I couldn't drink too little because I'd get dehydrated.

And there was a big, long list of foods I had to avoid.

Plus I had a handful off pills to take every morning and evening. I was now well established as a patient whose kidneys had failed.

No Such Word As Can't

DESPITE it only being a few moths ago that I'd completed my Ironman, it now felt like a million years ago. I was now on dialysis eight hours a night, every night. I was taking more pills than Bez and Shaun Ryder in their heyday. I felt exhausted all the time. And I was ready for bed at 9pm each night.

I could still go out and meet friends but I couldn't drink much. I could go out for meals but would have to avoid most of what was on the menu. In fact, the only thing I could still do that my condition hadn't affected was go to the cinema. So that's what Julie and I did. Most weekends, we'd go. Just for a couple of hours, I could completely forget about everything.

One night, while I was booking tickets to see a film, my e-mail pinged. It was an advert for a local 10km. There was a time when I could do this distance before going to work without batting an eyelid. But just finishing would take all my effort and willpower. But as you've probably guessed by now, I like a challenge, so I signed up.

I went back to hospital to meet my new nurse. The peritoneal dialysis nurse was called Caroline, a very happy, friendly nurse who was extremely positive about the fact I wanted to keep training despite being so ill. I asked her about doing the 10km and she said it was further than she could run but there was no real reason medically why I shouldn't do it. But she did remind me that I was actually really ill. She said: 'Just be sensible and you should be alright. If you feel sick, dizzy, out of breath or exhausted at any point, pull out.' I reminded her that this is how I felt all the time.

She smiled and said that this was probably true but to just be careful. I jokingly asked if I could have an extra shot of EPO to get me round. She pulled a face and shook her head. As I was getting ready to leave Jude, the nurse who first told me the bad news, popped in. She asked how I was doing and Caroline told her I was racing again next week.

Jude's face fell as she asked if I was doing 'another Iron thingy'.

I reassured her that I was just doing a local 10km.

She looked at me with an expression of disbelief and said under her breath said: 'Incredible…well, take care and good luck.'

I thanked both of them and left to head back into work, feeling a bit better than I had done in the last few weeks. What's more, I had another goal. So, it was only 10km and I'd probably come last but I didn't care. I was going to be racing again.

While all this was going on, the hospital were organising for my brother to come down to Guy's Hospital to start his tests. This would take over six months. But now I was on dialysis, it became a bit more urgent.

I had since found out that my dad's blood pressure would have been too high for him to be an option. Besides, both my parents were in their 70s. My mum was still quite active for her age but with a brother just 18 months younger than me they decided that they'd test him first and go from there.

What my brother was prepared to do for me was amazing. There's the medical risks and the fact he'd have to take a minimum of eight weeks off work. Plus, he'd have to spend quite few days travelling down from Barnsley to hang around

Guy's Hospital all day while they poked, prodded and tested every part of his body to make sure he was OK to donate. The testing was extremely rigorous but the last thing they wanted to do was take a kidney out of someone who wasn't 100 per cent fit.

The first thing he'd have to do was provide a passport picture and birth certificate to prove that we were related. Before a donor gets the go- ahead, it's not just all the physical tests they must pass. They also have to have an interview with someone from the transplant board. It's their job to check that nothing untoward is going on.

By this, I mean that they'd check he was actually my brother and not just some guy off the internet that I was paying. It's illegal to sell organs in this country. They'd also check that he had volunteered and that he wasn't being pressured into it.

This was actually quite funny because, despite the fact there's 18 months between us, people think we look almost identical. So when we met the woman from the transplant board, it was a very short interview. She spoke to me first, then my brother, then both of us together. She said that everything seemed fine and my brother was given the all-clear to be tested to see if he was a match and could donate.

We'd made it over the first hurdle.

Meanwhile, I continued to focus on my new race. Starting to train for a 10km while on dialysis was a mission. I couldn't run with the fluid in, so I had to finish work, go downstairs to the showers, hook myself up to another bag, drain the fluid out (which took about 30 minutes) and dispose of the used fluid. Then I'd have to go for a short run to the station, get home and drain the other bag of fluid back in (this also took about 30 minutes) so that could work for a few hours before going to bed.

Before getting into bed, I'd have to plug myself back into the machine, which again took about 30 minutes. It wasn't painful at all but it was a bit of a faff. I never slept particularly well, either. It was hard to get used to being plugged into a machine while you slept.

My running was now painfully slow. But I refused to give up. It took all of my willpower to get out and run. But it was worth it. Afterwards, I felt good. I kept this up for next few weeks and incredibly, I was starting to get fitter. The human body really is an amazing creation. It can put up with a hell of a lot.

With only a week to go, I wanted to test if I could actually run his distance. I got up on a cold foggy November morning. Before I could go anywhere, I had to go through the usual routine that I was now used to but there were no shortcuts. It made a quick exit from the house impossible.

First I'd get up, unplug everything from the night before and dispose of all the tubes, waste liquid, valves etc that plugged into the machine. Then I had to sterilise everything. But this was just the beginning. To have a shower, I'd have to cover the exit site, where the pipe came out, and make sure it was completely sealed off so no water could get to it.

Once out of the shower, I'd remove this covering, sterilise the area around the sink before laying all the stuff out. Then I'd put on some medical gloves, carefully clean around the tube sticking out of my side (it looked as weird as it sounds) before putting on a new dressing. I'd fold the tube back on itself and tape it down so it didn't stick out. Then I'd be ready to go.

An hour later, I left the house. I slowly ran off up the road and towards a local park. I still found running incredibly therapeutic. I know that exercise releases endorphins in the brain and that's why you feel good after doing it. But I had no idea why running, cycling, swimming or any exercise for that matter seemed to clear the mind. No matter how bad things are, a brief spell of exercise helps you forget about worries and stress completely, if only for a short time.

However, all I could think about on this particular run was how tired I felt. My legs felt like lead. It was like I was running through treacle wearing lead shoes and very heavy hat. I tried a brief sprint but there was nothing there. I slowly made progress trudging up the hill until I got to Blackheath. This was my 5km mark, so time to turn round. The journey home was easier. I could do this. After one hour and five minutes I finally got back home, 22 minutes slower than my healthy 10km PB. But at least I knew I could complete it, without walking.

The race was on a Sunday and was organised by a local athletics club. It was only a short drive from my house. So after some breakfast, I set off. I pulled up at the venue and it was a crystal clear winter's day. There had been a slight frost but the sun had melted most of it. It was perfect weather for a race.

We all lined up behind the starting line and the gun went off. There was the usual jockeying for position at the front but I was at the back, so it didn't affect me. The single goal I had was to finish. (And hopefully not come last.)

The club runners in their teams' colours were long gone. Then there were the serious runners who didn't belong to clubs but still ran like gazelles. Then there were the casual runners followed by a group of overweight and out-of-breath runners, who were there to just get round. And finally, at the back, there was me.

A lot of the people in the last group were probably running for the first time. This would be the beginning of their journey to losing weight, getting fitter and being happier. I guarantee a few of them would go on to run marathons as they fell in love with the feeling you get.

Others would get home, light up a fag, burn their trainers and chuck their kit in the bin before going to the pub and swearing never to do anything like that again. But they would definitely be in the minority.

I made it round the first 8km at a steady pace. (And by steady, I mean incredibly slowly.) I was close to the back but I wasn't last. I stopped to get some water as my mouth and throat were painfully dry. This made me feel a bit better. My legs felt OK but despite taking huge lungfuls of air I still seamed out of breath. There just wasn't enough oxygen going round my body.

By now, most of the other runners had long since finished. Some had probably picked up their medal, driven home, had a shower and were now sitting on the sofa checking their times on the results page on their laptops. But some of us were still running.

The final 400m was on a running track. I tried for sprint finish but, again, the tank was well and truly empty. I slowly jogged over the line and looked behind me. Much to my relief, there were a few people behind me. Not only had I finished, I hadn't come last.

I got my medal and headed back to the car. I had to get home to fill myself back up with the fluid I needed. Not the most exciting way to celebrate – but, as they say, 'them's the breaks'.

Once back at home, I reflected on what I'd just done. I felt tired on the run and out of breath but I didn't collapse over the line. If I had to, I could have carried on running. I started to wonder how far I could go. I reckoned I could probably do a half-marathon. Again, it would be incredibly slow but why not. It would be possible, Wouldn't it?

Dark Days

I WOKE up and went through the usual routine. Unplug, sterilise, wash, sterilise... but this time when I cleaned around the exit site of the tube, I noticed it was red and inflamed. I tried to clean it but it was really sore. The tube in my side had got infected. This was the last thing I needed, especially because it was a Sunday. I rang the hospital and they said there was nothing they could do until Monday. But in the meantime, I should go to my local A&E.

Great. A&E, the place where time stands still and every drunk lunatic from a 40-mile radius goes to hang out and shout at the doctors and the nurses. One time in A&E, I'd even seen a drunk guy shouting at a bin because he'd been kept waiting. This was going to be one long afternoon.

I asked Julie to drive me there as my side was now really sore. She didn't complain but I'm sure she was just as excited as I was about heading off to spend the day in a real-life version of *One Flew Over the Cuckoo's Nest*. We arrived at the hospital and parked up.

We slowly walked to reception and registered. The woman behind the counter informed us that we'd be seen in about seven years' time– or some wait to that effect. We took a seat and prepared to sit around for hours. Surprisingly, it was quite quiet. There weren't many drunk people there, either.

There was young kid who looked like he'd broken his leg playing football, a woman whose hand had been badly burnt and an old guy who was asleep. At least I hope he was asleep. He'd probably arrived when he was a teenager and had been waiting ever since.

I went off to get something to drink, more to pass the time than anything else. We'd only been there about 45 minutes and I was already bored to tears. I walked off down a never-ending corridor trying to find a vending machine but after a while I gave up. I returned to see Julie talking to a nurse.

I couldn't believe it. We'd only been there three quarters of an hour and they were ready to see me already. It turned out that this was just the first check-up. I had to see a nurse who would assess me. Then if I wasn't at death's door, I'd go back outside and wait to see a doctor. The nurse looked at the hole in my side and concurred that it did look like it was infected. She said a doctor would probably prescribe me some antibiotics then I'd go home. But to be on the safe side, she'd still like a doctor to have a proper look.

I had to wait another three hours to see a doctor, who told me that it was indeed infected. He wrote me a prescription. He also said I should go to the renal department at Guy's first thing in the morning. But at least if I started taking the antibiotics now, they could get to work straight away, stopping the infection getting any worse.

He handed me the prescription and we went off to wait in the pharmacy. As we waited, a guy who had a crazy stare sat next to me. He looked like Kramer from *The Seinfeld Show*. He just sat there staring at me. Eventually, I turned to meet his gaze. He asked me why I was here. As I explained, he nodded slowly and stroked his chin, like he understood. He then proceeded to tell me why he was in the hospital.

He told me that he'd had a bad accident while base-jumping. (He didn't look like your typical base jumper.) He told me that he'd nearly broken his back while leaping off the roof of Matalan, in Lewisham, and he was waiting for some 'horse pills', as he called them. This wasn't the end of the crazy story, either. He said that he didn't actually have a parachute because they're too expensive, so he just used a load of plastic bags. As I mentally pictured this guy jumping off the roof of Matalan with his homemade parachute, my number came, just in time. I got up to collect my antibiotics and made a sharp exit.

I nodded goodbye to Lewisham's answer to Bear Grylls and left the hospital as fast as I could. The first thing I had to do was go and pay for the car park. I posted the card in the machine and... Jesus Christ! £24! There are members of the Corleone family who would have been proud of this level of extortion. I'd get a helicopter next time – it would be cheaper.

The next day, I got up and caught the train into work. I was pretty used to feeling awful by now. I was so tired all the time that I welcomed my 25-minute commute, so I could get some extra sleep. My train pulled into Charing Cross and a kindly old man woke me up. I got on the tube and fell asleep again. But luckily, I woke up just in time to get off at my stop.

I got into work and called Guy's Hospital straight away. I explained what had happened and the nurse said I should come in now. I shut my laptop down after being there for a whole ten minutes, apologised to Al – again – and headed off.

Working with a partner is great but when you have to have time off, you really feel like you're letting them down. But we were good mates and we has a kind of motto. 'Health and family first'. No matter how busy you are, if one of you needs time off for one or the other you just deal with it. And it's worked both ways. Al's wife had a terrible eye infection that left her blind in one eye. Whenever he needed to go to hospital with her – whatever was happening at work – he'd go and be with her.

An eye infection doesn't sound that serious but believe me (and I'm sure she won't mind me saying this) it was horrific. It was caused by a water-borne amoeba getting behind one of her contact lenses. This led to years of treatment and resulted in a corneal graft (transplant). She has since campaigned to add a warning to the packs of contact lenses that highlight how dangerous it can be if you get them wet, hopefully saving the sight of thousands. She has even won the Health Campaigner of the Year award, which she picked up at the House of Commons.

The fact that getting your contact lenses wet could cause you to go blind was a particular worry to me (and no doubt thousands of other triathletes) because I often swam in my lenses. I now only use prescription goggles. It's a pain – but nothing compared to the agony of what she went through.

Rock Bottom

I ARRIVED at the hospital and went straight upstairs to see Caroline, my dialysis nurse. She looked at where the infection was and delicately felt the area around it. She said the first thing to do would be to inject antibiotics into the bags of fluid that I drained into and out of myself each night. I'd also need to do an extra 'exchange' during the day. This meant halfway through the day at work, I'd have to drain everything out, inject the antibiotics into another fluid bag and then drain it back in again.

This was possible but it wasn't something that filled me with joy. The doctor came in to check on me and he agreed that this was the best course of action. I asked what would happen if the infection didn't clear up. He said they'd have to remove the tube completely and then put me on haemodialysis.

My heart sunk. I knew that this would require another two operations. One to remove the current tube I had sticking out of my side and the second to put in the new one in my neck. Plus, haemodialysis would mean I'd have to come into the hospital three times a week for four hours at a time. The machines that do this are huge, so unless you plan to be on it for a long time, you have to do it in the hospital.

The doctor gave me a prescription and I trudged downstairs to the pharmacy. I queued up for ages waiting for my number to come up. It was like the world's slowest, most depressing bingo hall. Finally, I went up to collect a huge bag of vials filled with antibiotics. I was also given a box of pills to take. The pharmacist told me that I would have to go back upstairs to collect a load of syringes. (Weirdly, the thing that annoyed me most about this was that I was going to be even later for work.)

My rucksack was now full of drugs. It had the usual syringe in it for an EPO injection later that day. I had a bag in my pocket full of the pills that I had to take at lunchtime and now I also had 24 syringes and a sack of antibiotic vials.

I headed back into work and stuffed my bounty under the desk. We were called straight into a briefing to write a new advert for Cesar dog food. This was a welcome relief. You may find it hard to imagine but anything that made my life 'normal' was welcomed with opened arms.

Halfway through the day, I'd have to go to the shower, lock myself away, inject the antibiotics into the fluid bag, drain out the old fluid and drain the fluid back in. This took about an hour, so I did it at lunchtime. It only left me enough time to grab a sandwich before going back to work. It would never be classed as one of the great advertising lunches that the industry was famous for.

I repeated this every day for the next two weeks. Ten days into this treatment, I got gout again. I was beginning to feel broken. The fight was slowly being knocked out of me. I was cold and tired most of the time. I seemed to spend my life doing fluid exchanges. I had to watch everything I ate and everything I drank, and now gout had decided to pay me another unwelcome visit.

As I lay their trying to block out the agony, I heard a knock at the door. I got out of bed, being careful not to let anything touch my toe, and limped downstairs. I was taking so long, they knocked again. Each step caused me to wince in pain. I finally got to the front door and the person doing the knocking had just started to walk away. I called them back.

A very earnest-looking guy in an ill-fitting grey suit looked at me and smiled. He told me he was from some church, with a name that I can't remember. He wanted to know if he could come in for a chat. Had I really spent the last two minutes limping down the stairs to be bothered by this fool? I sighed and said thanks but I wasn't interested. As he walked away he called out: 'Remember Jesus loves you.' He's got a f*cking funny way of showing it, I thought to myself as I limped back inside the house to get ready to go back to hospital to be told I'd need another operation.

I hobbled into hospital feeling particularly down. There was light at the end of the tunnel because I had the option of a transplant. But at this present moment in time, it seemed like a very long tunnel and the light was nothing more than a dull glow.

Deep down, I knew what the outcome of this visit would be but I didn't really want to think about it. The doctor called my name and I went into one of the private rooms. I laid back on the bed and pulled up my shirt.

Looking down at the pusy mess, the doctor turned his nose up. It's not the most reassuring reaction I've had from a medical professional. 'Yes, this is quite badly infected. I'm sorry but it's going to have to come out,' he said.

He explained that they'd tried everything but the trouble was the antibiotics couldn't stop the infection growing on the plastic pipe itself. If it spread to my peritoneal cavity, it could infect my blood. This would turn an inconvenient problem into a life-threatening one.

The doctor asked the nurse if there was a room on the Richard Bright renal ward because I needed to go up there straight away. I was guessing that if I had this tube removed, I'd have to go on haemodialysis.

This meant I'd have to have a neckline fitted. The doctor told me that it was a pretty straight-forward operation and I'd only be in for one night. Plus, it would heal pretty quickly, too, so I could be back at work within a few days.

He also said that while my brother was being worked up to be a donor, I should come into Guy's to have my 'haemo'. My first session would only be for two hours. The second would be three and, finally, if it all went well, I'd have three four-hour sessions three times a week. But I could sort all that out with dialysis nurses later.

The doctor said the first thing to do was 'whip out the old pipe and plumb in a new one'. Eloquently put, I thought to myself. Still suffering with agonising gout, I hopped off to the lift with the nurse, so she could book me in and find me a bed.

I thought I'd be there for hours but there was already a free bed waiting for me. I was just glad to take the pressure off my foot as it was killing me. The nurse gave me something for the pain, I got on the bed and fell asleep. I'd already called Julie, who said she'd come by after work with some food and to see how I was.

I woke after a few hours sleep to be greeted by two incredibly attractive young female doctors. They explained that they were training at the medical college over the road and they needed to practice examining patients.

Was this really happening or was I dreaming? It was like the beginning of a bad (or good, depending on your taste) porn film. Hardly surprisingly, they didn't strip off. They just poked and prodded me. I've no idea what they were looking for but they seemed happy with their work. They thanked me and went off to the bed next to me to prod someone else.

As soon as they'd gone, I drifted back off to sleep, only to be woken up by a nurse taking my temperature and checking my blood pressure. She told me that I'd probably be operated on tomorrow but someone would come round to check on me and explain what was going to happen and when.

For next couple of hours, I tried to get the TV contraption that hung over the bed to work. I entered my card details and, of course, it didn't work. There was a phone attached to it, with a helpline number on it, so I called that. That didn't work, either.

I asked one of the passing nurses to help and she took the phone receiver and then gave it an almighty whack. I couldn't imagine she'd be giving up the medical profession for a job in IT any day soon but I tried it again and it worked. Don't underestimate the incredible healing hands of an NHS nurse.

I was put through to a call centre in India and the guy on the other end of the phone took my card details, so I could watch the TV. This would at least alleviate some of the boredom of sitting around all day, although having said that it was the middle of the day and staring at the blank screen would have been just as exciting as watching daytime TV.

Eventually, a doctor came over to me and explained what was going to happen. I was booked for the first operation of the day, tomorrow. They'd remove the old tube and put a new one in my neck then within a week I'd be ready to start haemodialysis. He asked if I had any questions. I just asked if I'd feel any better on 'haemo' than on my current dialysis.

He told me that 'haemo' was a slightly more aggressive type of dialysis, so I might be left feeling a bit drained. But having said that, a lot of patients say they feel better on 'haemo' in the long run.

That night, I slept terribly. Hospital wards are the noisiest places on earth. Firstly, there's all the machines. The guy next to me had just come back from theatre and all the machines he was wired up to were making so much noise that it sounded like R2D2 was having a domestic with his wife.

There was a guy on the other side of me who was making all kinds of odd noises. I'm not sure what he was doing but he kept making the sound of a wellington boot being sucked out of a muddy bog. Then there was all the usual coming and goings of the nurses taking blood pressure, temperatures, dishing out pills etc.

Just as I was about to doze off, I heard a huge metallic crash. A nurse had tripped up and dropped all the equipment she was carrying. A few other nurses came over to help her. At least if she'd hurt herself, she was in the right place to be looked after. I'd have got a better night's sleep on Runway 4 at Heathrow.

I awoke at 5am, slowly blinking in the bright halogen lights as the ward woke up. I stretched and yawned as a nurse appeared by my bedside to do all my pre-op checks and fit a cannula to my hand. In my tired state, it took me a while to realise that this was the same nurse I'd seen yesterday. She must have been working for about 13 hours. Despite this, she still had a friendly smile for me. I'm not sure how happy I'd be after working 13 hours straight though the night.

It wasn't long after this that the porter came to collect me and take me to the operating theatre. I wasn't that worried about the operation itself. I just wanted it over with so I could try and get back to normal – although normal was beginning to feel like a distant memory.

Lying on the operating table, I slowly counted back from ten as the warm wave of anaesthesia gently rippled over me, sending me into a deep deep sleep...

I rubbed my eyes as I slowly came to. Julie was sitting by my bedside reading a magazine. She asked if I was OK. I didn't really know. I smiled a drunk smile and asked if the doctor had said anything. Just as I said this, he appeared with a clipboard and said the operation had been a success.

I reached up to my neck to feel the new tube that been fitted. It felt weird, almost like it would tear if I moved my head. So I sat there looking round the room like an Action Man with 'eagle eyes'. The doctor laughed at this (thanks) and said it would loosen up in a few days, so moving my neck would become much easier.

He also said that I should rest for the remainder of the day and, providing everything was OK, I could be discharged that night. Julie stayed for a few more hours before going home. With a few more hours to kill, I started reading a copy of *Triathlon Plus,* a magazine I'd brought with me.

One article caught my eye. It was in a section called 'Inspired By'. I can't remember the exact story but I remember the gist of the article. Each month, they'd write about a triathlete who had overcome some terrible accident or disease or had lost huge amounts of weight to race their dream race.

While I'd been ill, I often wondered how I could get more people to sign up to be donors. Maybe I could use my story in the magazine to ask more people to sign up. Doing this type of thing didn't really sit with my personality. I didn't really like talking about my achievements (the irony of you reading this statement while you're reading this book isn't lost on me). But the more I thought about it, the more it made sense. Even if one person signed up to be a donor, it had to be worth it. When I got home, I'd email them a brief outline of my story to see if they'd be interested.

For the next few days, I found 'the normal' I was looking for. Nothing remarkable happened at all. It was great. I got up, went to work and actually spent more than five minutes at my desk. One night, Julie and I went out for dinner and then to the the cinema to see the new Muppets movie. I'm normally into quite dark, disturbing films but I'd had enough of that going on in my own life, so it was nice to get a bit of light relief.

* * * * *

The day I started haemodialysis was the lowest I've ever felt. The night before, I'd spoken to my brother and he'd said they'd found a tiny stone, or a 'fleck' as they called it, on one of his kidneys. My first thought was 'God, what if he had the same problems as me?' He'd have to go through all this, too. I also selfishly thought this would mean he couldn't donate. The light at the end of the tunnel was in danger of being switched off completely.

They wanted him to do a 24-hour urine collection to see if there were any problems. Again, more inconvenience for him. Plus, he was also probably quite worried about it himself.

Up until now, I'd assumed everything would be OK. He'd volunteer, he'd be fine and we'd get on with it. For some reason, it took this bit of news to make me really think about what he was doing. We'd had all the interviews and they'd said the risks were minimal to the donor (there's a 1/3,000 chance of death). You actually had more chance of being killed just going about your daily business.

I started to think, what if something happened to him? I couldn't live with myself. I mean, how would you feel? I would be responsible if anything went wrong. I knew that he knew the risks and I got a little comfort from thinking that if the situation were reversed, I'd do exactly the same for him. But at this moment in time, this thought did little to allay my fears.

I sat on the chairs at the reception of the haemodialysis unit watching the other patients arrive. They were all elderly. This was mainly because if you have dialysis in a hospital, chances are you're high risk. Others patients either get it done at satellite units near where they live or people who will be on dialysis for a long time have the machines delivered to their homes.

The doctor said the only reason I was there was I wouldn't be on it for long. Hopefully, my brother would be matched any day. But after hearing my brother's news, I wasn't convinced that this would be the case. I continued to watch the other patients arrive.

A middle-aged guy with no legs was wheeled in past me in a wheelchair. I later learnt his kidney failure was caused by diabetes. Another complication of diabetes can be ulcers that, if left untreated, can damage limbs so badly that they need to be amputated.

He was followed by a couple of blind ladies who had also suffered complications from diabetes. They were followed by a group of other elderly people who all looked grey and lifeless. Two of them were so weak that they were slumped in their wheelchairs, fast asleep.

It felt like I'd hit rock bottom. It couldn't get any worse than this. At the time, I saw myself as just like them. They were a lot older than me. They had limbs missing and had lost their sight – so in reality we were worlds apart. But at this moment, it didn't feel like it. Normally, I'd be looking on the bright side. Thinking, well… it could be a hell of lot worse. But at this moment, I lost my optimism.

I gazed into space expressionless. I felt numb.

Everything I'd worried about had now happened, from the time I first looked up kidney disease on the internet to the first time I saw the old guy on dialysis in hospital.

The gout attacks. The missed races. The swelling in my ankles. The feeling tired all the time. The constant fluid exchanges. The EPO injections. The feeling sick. Feeling freezing cold all the time. The infections. The drugs I had to take. All the operations. All of this was leading here.

This was it.

This was the first time I felt that kidney disease had finally got the better of me.

As much as I tried to stop my emotions taking over, I couldn't. I felt tears slowly fill my eyes, which I wiped away with the back of my sleeve.

In my mind, I could hear the voice of Del Boy from *Only Fools and Horses* saying 'pull yourself together, you big tart.' This strange thought made me smile to myself. But it did little to change how I felt. A nurse walked past and looked at me but I looked away, embarrassed at how I'd let my feelings get the better of me. I felt totally broken.

A bit later, one of the dialysis nurses came over and gently put her hand on my shoulder. 'I'll be with you in a minute,' she said, giving me a moment alone to gather my thoughts.

I climbed up on to the bed next to the dialysis machine. A young Filipino guy came over to help me set it up. He sounded like a Filipino Bob Hoskins.

Setting up the machine was easy. It took him about five minutes and it was entirely painless. All I had to do now was sit here for two hours and see how I felt afterwards. About an hour in, one of the old ladies had a funny turn and threw up all over the floor. A long-suffering, overworked and underpaid nurse cleared it up and cared for her. They really are modern-day angels. For next hour, I just sat there watching the world go by.

A tea lady turned up and I had a cup of tea. She also offered me something to eat. She said I could have anything I wanted as long as I wanted Rich Tea biscuits because that's all she had. I was assuming she could pack up and go home as soon as she ran out of biscuits because she gave me about 15. I had bugger all else to do for the next few hours, so I slowly worked my way through the lot.

With about half an hour to go, a very grumpy old guy wearing a trilby turned up. The staff nurse called out: 'Afternoon George, what kept you?'

George replied: 'It's all that c**t's fault! Boris fucking Johnson! The Albino, Billy Bunter, Tory wanker! This wouldn't happen if Ken was in charge. I told everyone this would happen when he took over. Twenty-five minutes waiting for a fucking bus! And I had to stand. London's overcrowded. That's the problem. And if Boris has his fucking way, it's only going to get worse. You mark my fucking words.'

Mani, the Filipino nurse, looked at me and smiled. He said: 'This is 'appy George. I hope you don't like Boris Johnson. In case you 'adn't guessed, he's not 'is biggest fan.'

Even in my current mood, where I was feeling desperately sorry for myself, George cheered me up. He was clearly crackers but he made me smile. Every time I saw him, he'd have another reason why Boris Johnson was ruining his life.

If the tea lady ran out of biscuits, it was Boris' fault. If the ward was too crowded, it was Boris' fault. Even if the weather was bad, he'd find a way of blaming Boris.

The last half an hour of treatment soon passed as I listened to George grumbling about one thing or another until eventually he dozed off. It was like being in a big building when the air conditioning is switched off. The ward suddenly fell into silence.

Mani unplugged me and took my blood pressure, pulse and temperature. He asked how I felt. I felt fine. I was expecting to feel terrible but I felt OK. I asked him if it would be all right to bike to the unit. Would it be safe to ride after four hours on dialysis? I explained that while I was having peritoneal dialysis, I'd kept riding. He said he didn't see why not. If I felt OK, I should be fine. Some people get cramps afterwards but these normally subsided pretty quickly.

As I was getting ready to leave the ward, a group of much younger people started arriving. They'd done a full day's work, had finished and then come to the unit for their dialysis. This made me feel a bit better.

After the ordeal of seeing elderly patients at their lowest ebb, this was a welcome relief. It made me realise that this wasn't the end. You could still live a relatively normal life. Yes, it would be hard and all the symptoms would still have to be dealt with and managed with medicine. But after that horrendous low of earlier, I started to revert back to my old optimistic self.

My mood was lifted further still when I got home. The writers from the magazine I'd contacted had e-mailed me back and said they'd love to cover my story. First, they'd send a photographer over to take my picture then the editor would give me a call to interview me. Some good might come out of all this after all.

Coping

AFTER a couple of weeks of dialysis, I started to get into a routine. I'd bike into work for 9am, leave work at 4pm to bike to Guy's Hospital, have a four-hour session on the dialysis machine then bike home. This would get me home about 10pm – just enough time to eat and then go to bed.

I did this on Monday and Wednesday. On Saturdays, I'd try and get to the hospital as early as possible to leave the rest of the weekend free. I'd started taking my laptop with me, too, so instead of listening to George blaming Boris Johnson for everything from the extinction of bees to closure of his local pub, I'd sit around and watch films.

The doctors had upped my EPO levels, which meant I'd started to feel better than I'd done in quite a while. The cloud of my brother's test results still hung over me but he'd now done his 24-hour urine test and he should be getting the results by the end of the week.

I started to realise that, apart from the symptoms I'd been dealing with, one of the worst things about the last month was that I was scared of what was round the corner. Things just kept getting worse. Now things had got as bad as they were going to, I could start to deal with it.

Things were looking up. But the highs in life are never far from the lows, as I was about to discover. A meeting had overrun at work and I was late leaving. This in itself was no big deal but the later I started the dialysis, the later I'd finish. I just wanted to get in, get it done and go home.

I got changed as quickly as I could, jumped on my bike and headed off across London to get to the hospital. Speeding down Embankment, I came towards some traffic lights. They turned amber as I sped towards them. Instead of slowing down, I tried to speed up. I thought I'd just made it in time. But the policeman standing a bit further down the road clearly had a different point of view.

The young policeman who stopped me was a very skinny, ginger, pale-looking guy with buck teeth. You didn't need to be a psychologist to understand how he'd ended up in this profession. His job finally gave him a chance to be in charge, to pay back all those people who'd regularly separated him from his dinner money all those years ago at school. Today, I was the lucky recipient of this ginger ninja's wrath.

After he'd flagged me down, looking a little like a flamingo having a panic attack, he started to lecture me. 'Do you know how many people die on London's roads…' Thinking quickly, I apologised and said I was in a hurry to get to dialysis at Guy's Hospital. The tone in my voice made it sound like being five minutes late could be life threatening. He looked at me quizzically and asked to see some kind of proof.

I fumbled around in my wallet and produced my NHS card. He looked at it, briefly, and begrudgingly waved me on. That was a close call.

I pulled up outside the hospital and locked my bike up. As I raced upstairs, I noticed my rucksack seemed lighter than usual. Then it dawned on me. In my rush to leave work, I'd left my laptop behind. This would mean four hours of doing nothing. I had my phone with me but the internet was so slow on that it would probably take me most of that time to connect to it. This was going to be one long, boring session.

It was quite an odd sensation, doing nothing. Our brains are constantly occupied by one thing or another. So having nothing to do at all was actually quite relaxing. It almost felt like I was meditating. I tried to clear my mind of thoughts. However, this 'deep relaxation' lasted about two minutes before my mind wandered and I ended up counting the ceiling tiles (there were 228, in case you're interested). I would have made a terrible Buddhist monk.

After four hours of slowly watching a clock barely move, it was time to go. Mani unplugged me. I thanked him and left. As I got to the exit, I noticed that it had started to pour with rain. The orange lights of the car park twinkled through the rain-soaked windows of the hospital reception. The strange urban beauty of this sight did little to raise my spirits as I knew this meant I'd get soaked riding home.

I ran outside to find my bike but it wasn't there. Had I locked it up somewhere else? No…it slowly dawned on me that it was gone. Someone had stolen it. Someone had actually stolen a bike from outside a hospital. How low can you get? After the initial anger had subsided, I went back inside to see if the security guard had seen anything. I walked into the office to find him with his feet up on his desk fast asleep, snoring.

The perfect end to a perfect day.

I walked to the station in the rain to get the train home. As I sat looking out of the window, I remembered that last year I'd got my bike insured. This meant I could buy a new one, a lighter one. This cloud wouldn't have a silver lining. It would have a carbon lining with a new set of wheels.

I contacted the insurance company and they confirmed that I was I covered. Surprisingly, they didn't ask many questions. I'd already got a crime number from the police, so all I had to do was send off the receipt from the initial purchase with the police note and they'd send me a cheque for the full amount.

Just two weeks later, I had a new Scott Addict R3, the same model of bike that Mark Cavendish rode (obviously, his was of a much higher spec and would have cost about £8,000). Hopefully, some his of speed would rub off on me.

I decided to put this to the test by going out for rides with the club again.

I was now riding with novices rather than killing myself in group one or going for longer rides in group two, but it was good just to get back out again. For the few hours I was out riding, apart from being massively out of breath and dropped at every small hill we came to, I felt good.

After one of these rides, I had to go home and get ready because the photographer from *Triathlon Plus* magazine was turning up. I had no idea what he'd want me to do. Stand proudly in my lycra tri suit while pulling my best Blue Steel face? I did hope not. The idea of doing this was to use my story to get people to sign up to the organ donor register to help ill people, not make them sick.

I heard a knock at the door and answered it to greet the photographer. He was laden down with equipment, cameras, tripods and reflectors, so I helped him in and made him a cup of tea. We talked briefly about what I'd been through and the race. He said he'd already had a few ideas about what he needed.

Unfortunately, my worries about looking a bit daft were well founded. He definitely wanted me in my race gear. To say I felt awkward while posing for a camera was an understatement. He took loads of photos. (I'm assuming his thinking was if he took enough, at least one or two might usable.) Some close-ups, some of me on the bike and some just standing. I had a brief look at some of the shots on the back of his camera.

Oh dear, since being ill and training, I'd lost a lot of weight and I'd started to look pretty ill. I looked less David Gandy and more Mahatma Ghandi but still it was for a good cause.

I thanked the photographer and he promised he wouldn't print any photos that made me look too ridiculous. As he left, right on cue the editor from the magazine called. I took her through my story, which was basically an abridged version of what you've read so far. She asked me loads of questions just so she could get the details right. It felt a little like I was being cross-examined in a court. But I guess the story had to be accurate.

Getting Worked Up

I SAT at my desk staring blankly at a computer screen. We'd just been briefed on a new project but all I could think about was Mark's results. This was the day I'd find out if he'd been given the all-clear. I desperately hoped this was the case.

The phone rang and I picked it up before it had even got to the end of the first ring. It was Mark – and he had good news. While the fleck hadn't gone from his kidney, they'd decided it was so small that it wouldn't prevent him from donating. What they'd decided to do was remove it during the operation. They'd take out his kidney, remove the offending fleck and then give the organ to me. I've never felt relief like it. It felt like a huge weight had been lifted off my shoulders. I physically felt myself snap out of the coma of uncertainty that had clouded my every thought for the last couple of weeks.

There was still a lot that could go wrong. Would the operation be a success? Would my body accept it? How would my brother react? Most worryingly, would the hospital food kill both of us?!

Mark arrived at my house with his girlfriend, Megan. They've since got married and had two children. But at this

161

movement they were still boyfriend and girlfriend. The plan was for him to stay with me for a couple of days before we both went to the hospital together. After the operations, they wanted Mark to stay with me for two weeks so if anything untoward happened, it would be easy for him to get to the hospital. Obviously, Megan wanted to be there, too, to look after him.

The date of the operation had been delayed a few times but it was now set – May 10. Unlike various people's birthdays, this is a date that I will never forget. It's difficult to put into words the gratitude I felt towards Mark. The hardest part is I'll never be able to repay him.

We'd chatted about this before. In one of the sessions Mark had with the transplant liaison nurse, she explained that it's not uncommon for people to give hugely expensive gifts to those donating because they feel such a debt towards the donor. She explained that it's probably best to tell the recipient to not even try. While this sounded a little odd, it kind of made sense. When you think about it, what's the price of life? You can't put a fiscal value on health.

But having said this, whenever we meet it's not difficult to work out who gets the first round in.

The next morning, one of the nurses called me and explained what the plan was. I was to go to hospital the day before the operation, have a late dialysis session then the operation would take place the next day. Mark could just turn up in the morning.

Although he didn't show it, Mark must have been pretty worried about the whole thing. For me, I was in and out of hospital every other day. I'd had numerous operations, anesthetics and other procedures, so it was all pretty normal for me – and, if everything worked out, I'd end up feeling much better.

But Mark was perfectly healthy. He'd visited the hospital a few times for various checks but he'd never been in hospital for anything major. In fact, as far as I could remember, he hadn't been to one at all. Now he was about to voluntarily go into hospital to have a major operation, all for my benefit.

Anyone who puts their life on the line to help someone else is, in my opinion, a real-life hero. There's no bigger gift one human can give to another. Health is the singular most important thing in your life. Nothing else really matters. Everything else is just a 'nice to have'. And you never really, truly understand this fully until it's been taken away from you.

I didn't know how I'd feel after the operation. The doctors assured me that I should go back to feeling 100 per cent. Because the body massively over-compensated by giving you two kidneys, you only need one to function normally. The single kidney just takes up the slack of the other. So, all your blood results should go back to normal. If you go for a blood test after a successful transplant, your results should look almost identical to someone with two kidneys.

This is obviously good news for the recipient but the same should be said for the donor. Their single kidney after a few days will do the work of two. Despite this extra work, there's no medical evidence that their kidney should wear out any quicker.

Despite only being a day away from the biggest event in my life, I was surprisingly calm about the whole thing. I don't know if this is a reflection of my personality or the simple fact that I'd had about six months to get used the idea. I think part of it was that I was actually looking forward to it. Not to the operation itself but to getting my life back.

That night, I packed ready to go to the hospital in the morning. As well as all the usual stuff, I took flip-flops, three pairs of tracksuit bottoms and some ear plugs. I'd read that flip-flops were the best things to wear after the operation because, with a huge scar across my abdomen, I wouldn't be able to bend down. The tracksuit bottoms were something else that proved to be a god send.

Wearing jeans would rub on the scar, so soft elasticated tracksuit bottoms would be much more comfortable. In fact, I found them so comfortable that I still wear them round the house today, much to Julie's annoyance and Al's amusement. Julie calls them my 'ASBO pants' and says they make me look like a petty criminal.

Al finds it amusing because, being a Scouser, he'd worn them for years and I always took the mickey out of him for wearing them. Now, after years of giving him stick, I was the proud owner of a pair.

The ear plugs were a token gesture to try and block out the noise, so I could try and get some sleep. I also took a my laptop, a load of DVDs, books and magazines. I was taking so much stuff it would look like I was moving in, not staying for a few nights.

The next morning, I woke up and it was a lovely spring day. The birds were singing and the first shoots of daffodils were starting to peek through the earth in the front garden. There wasn't a cloud in the sky. I hoped this was a good omen for what my brother and I were about to go through. I kissed Julie goodbye as she went off to work and said I would see her later.

My mum and dad were coming down to London that night and we were all going out for meal in a place near the hospital. I'd have to spend most of the day sitting around the hospital, getting loads of last-minute tests, so at least this would give me something to look forward to.

I took Mark and Megan up a cup of tea, said to Mark I'd see him later and then headed off to the hospital myself. I arrived at the renal unit to be greeted my liaison nurse, Christina. She explained what would happen today before my operation the next day.

The first thing I would do is meet my surgeon. She said he'd be up in a few minutes. As she said this, I heard a voice with a New Zealand accent ask if I was Diccon. I replied 'yes' and he reached out to shake my hand.

He said: 'Hi, my name's Chris Callaghan and I'll be your surgeon tomorrow. How are you feeling?'

I told him I felt OK considering but was looking forward to trying to get my life back. He said he'd seen all my X-rays and that it should be pretty routine. I had no idea how many transplants he'd done, how many lives he'd saved and improved ten-fold but for him to tell me it would be routine reassured me greatly.

We chatted generally about my medical history and how lucky I was to be in a situation where I had the option of having a transplant. He shook my hand and said goodbye. I liked him. He had a great bedside manner. I know this would have little bearing on the actual outcome of the operation but it made a difference.

I went back outside to wait for my nurse to come and get me. She offered to help carry all my stuff but the gentleman in me wouldn't let a lady carry my bags. Even in this position, less than 24 hours away from a major transplant, a little part of me still wanted to show that I wasn't that ill.

I arrived at the Richard Bright ward and was shown to my bed. Another nurse took over and said that the empty bed next to me would be for my brother tomorrow. I started to unload all the stuff I'd brought with me. The nurse looked at me and raised an eyebrow. 'Planning on staying long?' she said with a rye smile. 'We like 'em in and out here, so don't make yourself too comfortable. Besides, in a few days, you'll begging to leave. It's madhouse here...'

I sat up on the bed and took in my surroundings. There were about 12 beds in total. At least four of the people there had already had the operation and were recovering. But the guy opposite me looked in a bad way. He had a tube sticking out of his nose and he was incredibly skinny and pale. The skin just hung from his face. If it wasn't for the fact he had his eyes open, I would have thought he'd passed away.

Everyone on this ward had kidney problems of some kind but I couldn't for life of me think what was wrong with him. As I pondered what had brought him here, another doctor came over and introduced himself and asked how I was settling in. Settling in? He made it sound like it was my first day at a new job. I told him I was fine. He explained that I'd have my last (hopefully) dialysis session that night. I was booked in quite late, so I'd be in the best health possible for the operation in the morning.

He told me my brother would go down first, so they could get his kidney out. Then, once his operation was well under way, I'd go down and they'd 'open me up' (I hasten to add this is my terminology, not the doctor's), so they could put my brother's kidney in me. They would then monitor me in a holding bay while my brother's kidney took up the job of my old ones. This was also where I would come round from the anaesthetic before going back on to the ward.

He said I'd feel very groggy and probably a bit confused when I came round. He went on to explain that I'd also be on a high level of painkillers, which can make you feel very lighted headed and almost drunk. I didn't tell him that I knew exactly what he was talking about – and that I actually enjoyed the sensation. I won't lie, morphine made me feel great. I wouldn't suggest doing it on a daily basis but the times I've had it in hospital, it made the whole experience much more enjoyable. It's the drug equivalent of a nice glass of red wine while sitting in front of a warm fire, wrapped in a blanket.

While I debated the merits of prescription drugs, I looked around at the other patients. I now had a few hours to kill while I waited for the anaesthetist, so I thought I'd wander around and chat to some of them, see how they'd got on. The first person I met was a guy called Andrew.

He'd had his operation two days ago and he said it was a breeze. He got up from his chair and showed me an enormous scar that was held together with what looked like metal clips. To show me how little pain he was in, he started jauntily walking up and down the ward. I was concerned he was going to break out into a dance as he was so happy and apparently pain free.

He went on to tell me that his new kidney hadn't kicked in yet but he was hopeful it would start soon. The doctors had told him it was just 'lazy' and it should start working within a few days.

I asked if he had any advice for me as I was having my op tomorrow. He said they'd give me the option of having an epidural, so I should take it. He said he couldn't feel a thing. After the op, he said he was 'running around the place like a kid at a wedding'. No pain at all. I found this hard to believe but the epidural sounded like a good idea. The less pain I was going to be in, the better.

I asked him where he'd got his kidney. Had a relative donated it? 'He looked down and was silent for a second.

He took a deep breath and shook his head.

From his reaction, I knew what he was going to say.

He told me it was a cadaver.

We both stood in silence for a moment when he said this as the gravitas of what had happened slowly sank in. Someone had died and they'd been generous enough to consider people like us while they were still alive.

There was someone out there who'd just lost a husband or wife, a mum or dad or a son or daughter. He said obviously he was over the moon that he'd had a chance to get his life back. But his excitement was tempered with the knowledge that someone had to have died so that he might live.

The next person I spoke to was a very smartly dressed guy in his late 50s (he was wearing burgundy pinstripe pyjamas and spoke like the Major in *Fawlty Towers*). His wife had donated. He'd been in about five days and was just waiting for the all-clear to go home. He told me, unlike the stories he'd heard, he hadn't woken up feeling amazing with a sudden rush of new life and energy. In fact, he didn't really feel any different at all. He said this as a nurse nearby said: 'Just you wait – you'll feel better soon. It will take a couple of months until all your levels are back to normal. But trust me, you will notice a difference.'

I spoke to most of the people on the ward and one thing was clear – there was no guaranteed outcome. How you feel afterwards varied massively. There was Andrew, who despite the fact his transplanted kidney had yet to start working was dancing around like Fred Astaire. Then there was the Major, whose kidney was working fine yet he hadn't noticed any difference. I went back over to my bed and lay down. I thought I may as well get some sleep to keep my strength up. Just as I closed my eyes, the anaesthetist showed up.

She looked over all my charts and explained what aesthetic she'd use. She told me how I'd feel, what the process would consist of and what to expect. She was accompanied by more doctors, who checked my notes, too. The NHS gets a lot of stick but I really felt like I was in excellent hands. People talk about the postcode lottery for which hospital you get. Well, having ended up in Guy's, I definitely felt like I was one of the winners.

I asked about the epidural and she said that it was an option. There were some dangers involved but it would mean I would suffer from a lot less pain. This sounded to me like a risk worth taking.

Eventually, they all left me alone and all I had to do was wait until my brother, mum and dad, Julie and Megan turned up so we could go out for something to eat. It would be the last supper, as my brother called it. We joked about it but as the moment of truth slowly got closer, we were obviously getting more nervous.

During this time, I can't imagine what my parents were going through. For anyone who has kids, just imagine for a second how you'd feel if your child had to go for a life-saving operation. Now imagine the person saving their life is your other child, who also has to go through a serious operation. There can't be many instances in which two of your children will have big operations on the same day.

All the reassurance in the world wouldn't stop you from worrying that maybe, just maybe, something could go wrong.

My mum had already said she didn't want to see us the morning before the operation because she wasn't sure she'd be able to hold it together. She'd come and see us afterwards, once we were both back on the ward.

I sat about watching hospital life pass me by as I waited. The guy sat opposite me with the tube up his nose appeared to be getting sicker. An old African man from another ward wandered in with nothing on but a dressing gown that wasn't done up, leaving little to the imagination.

He was closely followed by the catering lady and what she had on offer would be even less appetising. But this didn't worry me too much, because I was going out. I'd already let the nurse know that I wouldn't need anything to eat. The NHS is hard pressed for funds as it is, without me ordering a meal that I wasn't going to be there for.

As the food filled the ward with the smell of a bin on a hot day, my family arrived, so we could go out. We'd booked a local place down the road, nothing fancy, but it would be nice to all meet up before the big day. I was tempted to have a beer but decided against it. The doctor had warned against having anything like steak or curry because the anaesthetic and the painkillers would block me up for quite a while, so they recommended something light.

I wasn't that hungry anyway, so opted for a small bowl of pasta. This is rare for me. The nerves must have finally started to get the better of me.

We finished up and said our goodbyes. I kissed Julie goodnight and said I'd give her a ring later. My parents, Julie and Megan walked off into the night and I headed back towards the hospital to have my last dialysis session. In just 12 hours, I'd be on the operating table.

The Gift of Life

I WAS woken up at around 6am. It took me a few seconds to realise where I was and what was happening. I rubbed my eyes and looked around. 'Morning,' said a voice next to me. I looked round to see my brother sitting on the bed next to mine.

Today was the day.

'You alright?' I casually asked.

'I've had better days,' he replied. 'I've been up since 5am. I'm knackered already. They told me I'm due to go down around 8am then you'll come down soon after.'

'Feeling nervous?' I asked.

'A little. But it's all so surreal it doesn't really feel like it's happening.'

'Yeah, I know what you mean. You could always not go ahead with it – and go for a pint instead.'

Mark smiled. "Hmm, tempting, maybe afterwards,' he said.

It didn't take long before Mark was surrounded by doctors and nurses checking various things. A nurse fitted a cannula to his hand. She gave him a gown and shut the curtains so he could get changed. I looked at the clock… only few hours to go now.

An hour later, a porter came to get Mark. As they whisked him off, he called back: 'See you on the other side.'

'Good luck,' I called after him.

After a nervous few hours, a nurse came up and said they were ready to remove my brother's kidney, so they'd take me down to the theatre so they could make the transfer.

Right, here goes, I thought to myself. The porter wheeled me out of the ward and promptly crashed the bed into the wall. He adjusted and crashed it into the other wall. I hoped the surgeons were going to be little more delicate.

Eventually, he managed to steer me into the lift, which took us down to the basement, where the operating theatres were. Once in the theatre, the anaesthetist I'd spoken to earlier came in. The first thing she'd give me would be the epidural.

She got me to sit on the corner of the bed and crouch up into a ball. This would open up the vertebrae in my back so she could inject the anaesthetic in a space that surrounded my spinal chord. This was relatively straightforward and didn't cause much pain. It worked surprisingly quickly. It wasn't long before I was almost completely numb in the area around my abdomen. She gave me a few more minutes before I was fitted with oxygen tubes up my nose.

She then placed a large pipe into the cannula on my hand and told me to count backwards from ten.

I had a strange sensation of my body filling with warm liquid as I counted down.

I've no idea what number I reached. This was the last thing I remembered before I slowly drifted off to sleep.

* * * * *

I woke up with a start. Everything seemed really bright, busy and noisy. I tried to focus on what was going on but everything was blurred. A doctor came over to me and asked if I was all right. All I could do was mumble something about pain. It hurt. Can I have some painkillers? Was Mark OK? Is he here? Pain…

I drifted back out of consciousness.

Up again I woke. I felt first thing pain. Confused feeling I am. Nurse I feel still can pain. What? I can still pain feel. And weird feel pain I…

The heavy dose of medication was leaving me disorientated and confused. I didn't really know what was going on…

It wasn't long until the warm, hazy sensation of morphine enveloped me in a cotton wool fuzz, leaving me, for want of a better description, high as a kite. They slowly wheeled me upstairs next to my brother. He sleepily looked up at me smiled. It was the woozy smile of someone who was also on a very high dose of pain medication.

Both my parents were there to greet me. They'd arrived earlier so they could see Mark. Through my purple haze, I could see they were both visibly moved to see their boys had made it through in one piece. I'd like to say that now was the time I said something deeply profound and moving to my brother. But the drugs had clearly messed with my brain. I mumbled something about geckos on wheels and fell back to sleep.

The next 24 hours were a bit of blur. I woke up occasionally to chat to Mark. But I've no idea what we talked about. Mark was on even stronger painkillers than me. Halfway through one of our spaced-out chats he'd press his pain button, which released more painkillers into system, causing him to slowly doze off.

By the next evening, the nurses encouraged us to get out of bed and, if we could manage it, start walking about. This was easier said than done.

During the operation, a number of new tubes had been fitted. I had a tube in my neck to help measure fluid volumes and give temporary dialysis if it was needed. I had a tube attached to my cannula that was giving me morphine. I had a drain tube that was sticking out of my side to drain away blood and fluid from where my new kidney had been placed. I'd also had urinary catheter fitted. This is small tube that passes down the urethra (the tube of the penis) into my bladder to help monitor the urine output of my new kidney (and yes, this was as pleasant as it sounds). I'm glad I was out for the count when this was fitted. Attached to the other end was a collection box so they could see how much urine my new kidney was producing.

Moving around with all these pipes and tubes took forever. I was like a fly stuck in a spider's web. Every time I tried to move, I became trapped by another tube. But eventually I managed to get out of bed. Within 36 hours, I was up and slowly walking around, dragging my drip full of drugs with me. Mark was finding it a little harder. The donor is typically in more pain. But he soldiered on.

He tried to get up and sit in the chair by his bedside. He felt nauseous so they gave him some anti-sickness pills. This made him feel faint, so they gave him some oxygen. Despite these setbacks, he was slowly getting better, too.

Forty-eight hours after the operation, the doctors were very happy with how things were working out. My new kidney had started to take up the slack of my old ones. In fact, it had gone into overdrive. They said I should drink as much water as possible because when the new kidney starts working, it goes a little crazy at first. They weren't kidding. To stop myself getting dehydrated, I had to drink a litre of water every two hours and even then I couldn't keep up. I had to have a saline drip fitted.

Mark's pain was now beginning to subside. While I was on morphine, he was on a drug called fentanyl, which was around 80 times more potent. So while this blocked out most of his pain, it also seemed to block out everything else. Every time he used it, he fell asleep. It left him feeling totally wiped out. But as his body began to heal, he was needing less and less.

On the third day, we could both get up and walk around the ward. We were both bent double, like little old men, but we were up and about. We even made it out of the ward, into the lift and to the newsagents on the other side of the hospital, although this took us about an hour there and an hour back.

When I got back to my bed, a nurse was waiting for me. She had come to remove the drain tube from where my transplanted kidney was. It was a long rubber tube that went about 15cm into my side. The worrying thing about this procedure was that she was going to do it while I was awake.

She told me to lie back and lift my top then slowly breathe out while relaxing. As I breathed out, she slowly pulled out the tube. Out of everything I had done, this was the thing that disturbed me the most. Watching her pull the tube out of the hole in my side, while I was wide awake, was an odd sensation. It stung a bit but considering how it looked it wasn't actually that painful. A small trickle of blood dribbled down my side, which she quickly mopped up before adding a dressing. Just as she left, the pharmacist turned up.

Up until now, the nurse had just brought me the pills I needed in a small cup. I paid little attention to them and just downed them all with a mouthful of water. This was the first time I'd realise the incredible cocktail of drugs I'd been taking. Over the next few months, they would be slowly reduced but at the moment there was a huge long list.

I had to take advagraf and MMF (these were both immunosuppressant drugs that would help stop my body form rejecting my new kidney).

There was prednisolone (a steroid). This gave me so much energy, I felt like I could run through walls

I had oxycodone, which was a painkiller (the nice happy drug), along with paracetamol.

I also had to take antibiotics to make sure I didn't get an infection.

There was amplodopine, which helped control blood pressure, but as my original doctor had told me it also had renal protective effect.

Plus there was 75mg of aspirin to make sure I didn't get any blood clots.

There were some drops I had to take called valacyclovir, which would stop me getting cold sores because, in a highly immunosuppressed state, this was a risk.

I also had to take an antihistamine because I'd since become allergic to the morphine I was taking.

Apart from the morphine, incredibly, I didn't have an adverse reaction to any of them. I was extremely lucky. The leaflet in the box listed literally hundreds of things that could wrong, anything from heart attacks to brain swelling. It sounded like it would have been less risky to tap-dance across a minefield than take them. But to be fair, the more extreme reactions were incredibly rare and, besides, what choice did I have?

Other patients in the ward weren't as lucky as me. The guy in the bed next to me had a horrific reaction to his painkillers. He woke in the middle of the night screaming that he could see his dead dad and that he thought snakes were coming out of the lights. It was horrible to listen to. God knows how it felt to experience this type of hallucinatory nightmare.

As we were both getting better, more friends started to come and visit. Some of them noticed straight away that I'd started to look better. My colour had started to come back to my face. Before the operation, I'd started to look a bit grey, a bit like John Major in the old *Spitting Image* series. But as my red blood cells slowly started to increase, I became a bit more 'pinky', as one of them described it, more like a slapped piglet. I was like an old TV set that had suddenly had its colour turned back up.

One of my visitors had brought me the triathlon magazine, *Triathlon Plus*. I started reading it and I realised how much I'd missed feeling fit and healthy. For the last year, I'd felt pretty rough. But thanks to my brother (and with a bit of luck), my life would eventually go back to normal. By normal, I meant getting up at 5.30am to go swimming, going for runs in the pouring rain while everyone was sleeping and going on bike rides that the average person would consider to be a long drive.

I could go to work and work a normal working day without having to leave early to go to the dialysis unit. I could go out for a drink and not have to worry that after half a pint I'd have to start watching my fluid intake. I could go out on sunny day and not have to dress like it was winter. I could eat what I wanted. I could even book a holiday. I felt an enormous sense of relief.

The doctors had warned me that it was very early days and my body could reject the new kidney. There were any number of things that could go wrong. But these worries were currently far from my mind.

As I flicked through the pages, I started to wonder if anyone with a kidney transplant had done an Ironman. Could I be the first? Could I be in the *Guinness Book World Records*? The more sensible part of my brain chipped in with 'Shouldn't you just calm down, relax and get better?' Maybe I should but this seed was now well and truly planted and over the next few months it was going to get heavily watered.

My brother's surgeon came over to his bed and asked with a smile: 'Are you still here?' It was now just four days after the operation and they were already thinking about sending us home. They said we'd both made incredible progress and going home would be good for us. If nothing else we'd finally be able to get some sleep and something decent to eat. They told my brother that he could probably go home the next day, just five days after the biggest operation of his life. I know I've said it before but the human body really is a remarkable machine.

They told me I could probably go the day after that. I couldn't wait. I'd already started to feel a bit better and my blood test results were beginning to slowly return back to normal. Day by day, I would slowly start to get my life back. But the next few months would be critical. I was on a high level of immunosuppression, so I would have to make sure I avoided anyone who was ill. I'd also have to watch what I ate. I couldn't eat unpasteurised cheese, milk or yoghurt, foods containing raw eggs (such as homemade mayonnaise) and undercooked raw meats, fish and shellfish. I was also told to avoid buffets, although I think this is pretty good advice for everyone.

As long I didn't get invited to a Japanese wedding with a sashimi buffet where there was a chicken pox epidemic, I should be all right.

I was also told that exercise would be important as steroids made it incredibly easy to put on weight. Another side-effect was they made you incredibly hungry. I had a big appetite anyway but I once I started them I had the hunger of a Sumo wrestler at an all-you-can-eat Chinese restaurant.

That afternoon, I said goodbye to my brother. Hopefully, I'd see him tomorrow. He was now free to go. I had a few more blood tests and checks to go before I was allowed to go but I could manage another 24 hours.

I caught up with one of the many doctors who had been looking after me and he said he was pretty certain that I'd be able to go soon. Besides, he said, they needed the beds. They couldn't have healthy people taking up the space when sick people needed them.

He was joking but he was right. I was going to slowly become 'healthy' again. At that moment, I felt like someone had turned up a dimmer switch to full brightness. The clouds were clearing and the storm was passing by. I suddenly felt a rush of optimism. This was my second chance. I could do anything. The world would be my oyster.

The doctors had told me that I must take an absolute minimum of six weeks off before I went back to work. But an ideal amount of time would be whenever I felt completely better. Not just OK but 100 per cent better. That afternoon I said goodbye to Mark, gave him a big hug, thanked him again and said that I'd never forget what he'd done for me. I owed him my life. With any luck, I'd be joining him at home tomorrow.

Everyone had now been to visit, my mum and dad had gone home and it gave me time to reflect. I just sat on my bed for hours, thinking. Thinking how lucky I'd been. Thinking about the future.

I walked out to the lifts and decided to go to the top floor to see if I could see the view over London. Surprisingly, it was quite easy to walk about the hospital without anyone asking what you were up to.

Once at the top, I walked over to a large window and looked out over the sprawling metropolis. I stood gazing at the lights as the city hummed below me. Staring off into the distance, I reflected on what I'd been through. If I was lucky, the worst episode of my life was now behind me.

My moment was interrupted by a cleaner walking by with a bin bag that split and went all over the floor. He cursed loudly in a language I didn't recognise. I hobbled over to help him but I was still too sore to bend down. I apologised, lifting my T-shirt to show him my scar, and he waved me away, shaking his head as if to say 'Thanks, but I've got this.'

Back in the ward, a doctor came over and said that today's blood test results were good. My creatinine was dropping nicely. I was producing buckets of urine (a lovely image) and he couldn't see any reason why I shouldn't be able to go home tomorrow. I only had one question. When would I go to the toilet? It had now been six days. All the morphine had completely blocked me up.

The doctor fetched a nurse to come and talk to me. She said I'd already been given laxatives but if that wasn't working I should try drinking coffee. I explained that I hated coffee and that even the smell of it turned my stomach. She just told me to think of it as medicine. I was beginning to feel really bloated, so I was willing to give it a go, even if it did make me feel sick.

She returned with a small cup of coffee. I picked it up and smelt it. But instead of the repellent feeling of disgust, I weirdly quite liked the smell of it. I sniffed it again. I now liked how it smelt. It had a rich, deep aroma that I actually found quite pleasant. Weird. Then it struck me. Mark loved coffee. Could it be possible that, because of the operation, I'd taken on his love of coffee? (What was even stranger was this wasn't coffee made from freshly roasted beans, it was a simple cup of the NHS's finest.)

I'd read about people who've had a stroke coming round and speaking in a different accent. For example, there was a woman from Birmingham who'd had a stroke and when she woke up she spoke with a French accent. But I'd never heard of anyone's tastes changing after an operation.

I thought at the time it might just be the drugs – but to this day I now love coffee. It's really weird. I have no way of explaining it. I can also report that the coffee worked – and quite spectacularly.

The next day, I woke up to the usual chaos at 5.30am but this didn't bother me because I knew I was going home today. The nurse told me that the hospital had taxis to take patients home. All I had to do was go to the rank downstairs and there would be a driver waiting for me. I packed all my stuff up and got ready to go home. One of the nurses gave me a hand and helped me downstairs.

I opened my front door, walked into the living room and flopped down on the sofa. I let out a large sigh, relieved to be back in the comfort of my own home.

For the next two weeks, Mark and I did very little. We'd get up, take our painkillers then lie around on the sofas watching daytime TV and films. Each day, we'd go for walk, trying to go a little further each time. I started to note down everything I did. I wondered how long it would be before I could ride and run again. As much as I wanted to push myself again, I had to be sensible. I didn't want to give myself a hernia.

I still had to go to the hospital every other day for the first week and then three times the following week. Each time, my creatinine got a little better. My haemaglobin was climbing up and slowly all my other blood levels were beginning to balance out. It was still early days but it was looking like the operation had been a success.

After a week or so, Julie suggested we go out for a meal, just somewhere local, but it would be nice for a change. It would be a chance for Mark and I to get out of the house as we were beginning to go a bit stir crazy. We picked an American place down the road. They did great BBQ pork ribs and the portions were huge. The one thing we hadn't taken into account was that our scars were still quite sore. The pressure of having a full stomach could be quite painful.

I had a full rack of ribs, chips and a large bowl of coleslaw. Mark had an enormous cheeseburger. As we finished and our food began to work its way down, the pain started. It was a dull ache at first but we knew we'd over-eaten, so it was only going to get worse. It would now be a race to get home to get our painkillers before we both ended up in agony.

We called a taxi and both hobbled out of the restaurant. We made it back home just in time to get to our pills. We wouldn't be doing that again in a hurry.

After two weeks, Mark was ready to go home. We were both now pretty much pain free. We could comfortably walk for about half and hour without any problems. In fact, I felt like I was nearly ready to go back to work. But the doctor told me this was bad idea. If caught a cold or flu off someone, it would massively set back my recovery.

With Mark now gone, I started to get bored. It wasn't like I could go to the cinema or head into town to go to a gallery. I still couldn't ride, run, or swim. In fact, I wasn't really supposed to be doing anything except sitting around and getting better. But this was easier said than done when you're on steroids.

They gave me so much energy that I kept finding myself doing jobs round the house. It gave me a kind of mania. I cleaned all the windows on the front of the house. I scrubbed the kitchen floor. I did the gardening. I had to keep stopping myself. But each time I sat down, I'd feel the urge to get back up and do something else. I was like a man possessed. It was like everything was on fast forward. But thankfully, after a month, they started to slowly taper the dose, so I could return to planet earth.

As the days stretched into weeks, I started to feel fully recovered. It was going to be too late to recover enough to do any kind of racing this year but I would definitely pick it up next year. I chatted to my doctors about this and they said there was no reason why I wouldn't return to full fitness.

They actually said I'd return to be much fitter. Even when I first discovered triathlon, I was already technically suffering from kidney disease, even if my symptoms were minimal. I looked at a few races to enter the following year. Switzerland Ironman 70.3 looked like a good option. The swim was in a crystal-clear lake, then you'd head off into the countryside and it finished with a run around the old town. It looked stunning.

I'd enjoyed all the races I'd done so far but none of them had been anywhere as beautiful as this. I couldn't actually enter it yet but it would be open in about six months, so I'd enter it then.

The next few weeks flew by. In between watching dodgy 80s films I recorded on ITV2 and manically cleaning the house, I sat around and did very little, which is just what the doctor had ordered me to do. I spoke to Mark regularly, checking to see how he was. He said he was feeling much better, too, but like me he was getting bored of sitting around doing nothing.

I now only had a week left before I was due to go back to work. I now felt better than I'd done in years. I didn't realise just how bad I'd felt at the time. Looking back, I could see I wasn't in a good way at all. I just ploughed on as if nothing was happening, almost ignoring the symptoms. I couldn't comprehend how I'd managed to train for a full Ironman while still working full time. It was pure willpower, sheer bloody-mindedness. I certainly wasn't in any physical state to be doing it.

On my last week I started going for longer walks, just a few kilometres at a time. My operation had coincided with the start of summer, so it was quite pleasant and I'd spent enough time cooped up indoors to last me a lifetime. By the end of the week, I could walk 5km without any problem at all. I was now ready to go back to work and ready to start training to get some kind of fitness back.

I asked the doctors if they thought it would be OK and they said it should be fine as long as I built up slowly. They suggested I gave it another month before I went swimming or went out on my bike. But walking would be fine. They said I should avoid the gym for a while longer because they didn't want weight training to give me a hernia where my scar was.

Hello Fitness, My Old Friend

I'D now been back at work for four months. I'd finally found the 'normal' that had seemed so far away for so long. Everything clicked back into place and I picked up where I'd left off. But more importantly, I was able to train again. I'd started doing the odd swim, I'd been out on my bike a few times and I'd organised to go to the Alps to ride Alpe d'Huez with a few mates in May.

I decided that now was good time to give Fran a call and start planning for next year. I told him I wanted to do a half-Ironman in Switzerland. He said because I was pretty much starting from scratch, it might be an idea to have a longer build-up to the race. Besides, he could stop me going crazy and doing too much too soon.

The race in Switzerland I'd decided to do was in an area called Rapperswill Jona. It sounded great. The swim seemed pretty straightforward. An out and back in a lake. The bike looked incredible. It set off from the lake and went up into the mountains but thankfully not too far. It was more of a flavour, with a respectable 750m climbing. The run was in and around the old town. There was a section on the run ironically called 'stairway to heaven'. After four hours racing, having to run up 80 steps would obviously be hell.

I spoke to Julie about it and showed her where it was and she suggested we stay for a few extra days, make a bit of holiday of it. So that was sorted. We'd go for five days. I'd race in the middle of it and then we could spend a few days relaxing. I booked it there and then. Well, I say I booked it. I actually contacted a company called Nirvana, who pretty much do it all for you. In fact, the only thing they don't do for you is the training.

Slowly, I could feel my fitness coming back. Fran felt comfortable pushing me slightly harder in the gym without having to worry that he might kill me. My cycling, running and swimming was better than had it been for ages. I had to be careful, though. Because I was now 'better', I had to watch that I didn't go crazy and start doing everything flat out. Thankfully, I had Fran to guide me. So I started with easy aerobic runs and cycle rides, and most of my swimming was technique focused.

Occasionally, he'd throw in some tempo sessions but most of it was easy. On one of these sessions, I decided it would be a good idea to do it through Deptford (yes, really). In my mind, I thought I'd gently run to Deptford Park, do the speed sessions there before gently running back to Lewisham, where I'd get a train home. But this wasn't exactly how it panned out.

As I ran to the park, I took shortcut through an estate. I ran towards a group of lads hanging around an alleyway. I tried to run round them but as I ran past one of them stepped back, knocking into me. Because I was running and he was stepping backwards, I accidentally sent him flying. One of them shouted after me. This was going to be a much faster speed session than I'd originally planned because they all gave chase.

I legged it through the estate and hurdled a wall. I looked back to see that most of them were chasing me. My adrenaline had now kicked in and I was flat out. But I had no idea where I was going. I took a sharp left and sprinted on.

I turned round to see that I was making some ground. I ran past some overflowing bins and out on to a main road.

I stopped to look left and right to plan my route. But as I caught my breath, I heard them shout after me. This race wasn't over yet. I ran out into a small park. On the right was a path down a canal. On the left was an alleyway. I quickly chose the canal path and sprinted flat out towards a main road. As I ran across the road a bus drove past, cutting them off.

Once on the main road, I suddenly recognised where I was and felt an entire new sensation. I was happy to find myself in Lewisham. The bus had caused enough of a delay for them to give up. I'd made it. I gasped for air as I got to the station. A woman standing next to me looked at me quizzically. I smiled and she slowly moved away form me.

That had been a speed session of a lifetime. Needless to say, it was also the last time I took that route home. From then on, I ran through Greenwich Park and on Blackheath. Much safer. In fact, as I look back on it, I've no idea why I thought running through a Deptford estate would be a good idea.

All my other training sessions were more successful. Occasionally I'd get a cold, which took me a while to shake off. I don't know this for a fact but I'm pretty sure it was due to my immunosuppression medicine. The cold was no worse than the usual bog standard virus but it took ages to go away. Fran insisted that I rest until it had gone and then rest a bit more. That's the great thing about having a coach. You know when to train. But weirdly, the biggest thing I've learnt is when to do nothing.

With everything going well, except for the odd hiccup, I would be in pretty good shape for my trip to the Alps. I was going with three of my best mates. Phil, the guy who'd joined on my first trip to Ironman UK 70.3; Mark, who'd I'd raced with in my early forays into triathlon and Rog, the guy who joined me on my first-ever race back in London.

It was a miracle Rog was fit enough to join us at all. He'd had nasty bike accident about five months before and now had a large metal plate in his leg. Even after all this time, he was still recovering. I had no idea how he'd get up Alpe d'Huez and then spend the rest of the day riding.

We flew from Luton to Lyon and then picked up a hire car. From there, we drove to a small town called Le Bourg-d'Oisans at the foot of the mighty Alpe d'Huez. This would have been an ideal place to stay but we weren't staying here. We were staying at a ski hotel about 15km away. When Phil booked it, he'd obviously just looked on a map and seen that our hotel was pretty close by.

But it was actually nowhere near.

We slowly drove up into the mountains. The roads twisted an turned and the switchbacks took us up and up and up. We were now so high that my ears started to pop. The roads slowly got thinner and if you looked out of the window you could see a sheer drop down to the valley, hundreds of metres below.

After what seemed like an eternity, we got to the top of the mountain where we were staying. It had taken us about half an hour to drive up it. The enormity of what it is to ride in the Alps was slowly dawning on us. We stepped out of the car into the thin, fresh, clean mountain air. As I breathed in, I could almost feel my lungs being cleansed from the London smog I forced them to breathe on a daily basis.

Then I noticed the view. It was incredible. It was a clear day and you could see right across the valley to the mountains opposite. As we looked up and back, we could see the summit of Alpe d'Huez. This is where we'd be heading tomorrow.

This is the most famous climb in cycling. Immortalised by the many battles from riders in the Tour de France, this was due in part to an Italian rider named Fausto Coppi. He attacked French rider Jean Robin 6km from the summit after they'd been side by side from the start of the climb. Because this was the first year motorcycle TV cameras had filmed Le Tour, this incredible battle was seen by millions and Alpe d'Huez became *the* climb of the Tour.

The crowds it attracted were also legendary. It's been reported that, on one stage, over one million people lined the 21 hairpins to the summit, although more conservative estimates claim it was more like 400,000. Although I sensed there would be far fewer people watching us do it, it would still be incredible to ride the same route as so many of the cycling greats. It would be like a tennis fan playing on Centre Court at Wimbledon or a football fan having a kickabout at the Nou Camp.

We checked in and decided it would be best to get an early night. This took some considerable willpower. This was the first time we'd all been away together since the last stag do – and that certainly didn't end with small beer, a bite to eat and an early night.

The next day, we woke early and went outside. We had to drive back down the mountain to a local bike shop to pick up our hire bikes. Phil had sorted it out and we'd hired top-of-the-range Pinarello Dogmas. For those not *au fait* with bikes, these are the bikes the riders of team Sky use. To buy, they're worth about £6,000 but to hire they were €45 per day.

The groupset would be a little more basic but the frames and wheels were as good as it gets. Why they thought hiring them out to us was a good idea was lost on me. The mechanic fitted our pedals to the bikes, adjusted them so they were set up for us and we were ready to go.

We slowly rode up the road towards the beginning of the climb, preparing ourselves to ride the famous 21 hairpins to the summit. From there, we would spend the next 14km riding up hill. It starts steep with a 13 per cent incline then levels out at an average gradient of 8.1 per cent. Not ridiculously steep but when you ride this for 14km it soon starts to hurt. As we stood back to looked up at what we'd let ourselves in for, the majesty of it took your breath away. It was strange. You could almost feel it. I'm guessing mountain climbers have a similar feeling. It's man vs mountain.

We all started off together but the shop had given us timing chips, so it was clear that we'd end up racing one another up it. The first few turns didn't disappoint. After just 15 minutes, we'd already climbed higher than any of the hills we go up on local routes. The sun was now cutting through the cool mountain air and it was beginning to heat up.

I thought I'd test the water and got out of the saddle to see if the others could keep up. Much to my relief they didn't give chase, so I headed up on my own. It was difficult to pace it because I'd never ridden anything like it before. I just rode on and hoped for the best.

Halfway up, my mind began to wander. Just a year ago, at this time on a Saturday, I'd been sitting in bed in Guy's Hospital going through another dialysis session. Thanks to my brother, I was now halfway up one of the most famous climbs in cycling. I'd come along way since those dark days.

I looked back to see if the others were anywhere close but I'd lost them. I got to what I thought was the top, so I gave it everything I had, sprinting for an invisible finish. I then realised that this wasn't actually the top. I had another one kilometre or so to go. The road was covered in graffiti from past races. The names read like a who's who of cycling folklore. I rode over a faded message written in Italian. It said something about Il Pirata, the nickname of Marco Pantani, one of the best climbers cycling has ever seen.

I'm sure the message hadn't been there since the mid to late 90s, when he'd dominated the mountain but the romantic in me liked to think so. After what seemed like hours, I reached the top. I was now 1,860m above sea level. I sat down and opened one of the energy bars I'd brought with me. As I bit into it, Mark appeared closely followed by Phil. Finally, not that far behind him, was Rog. The fact he'd made it up at all was incredible considering the state of his leg.

As he gingerly hopped off his bike, we enquired how he felt. He looked in a lot of pain. But it wasn't his leg. It was his buttocks that were causing him wince as he sat down. The seat on his bike had rubbed badly and blistered his bum cheeks. He lowered his shorts to show us the damage. In a very short time, the seat had rubbed so badly that he looked like a baboon that had ridden from Land's End to John O'Groats on a sand paper saddle. Even to this day, it's not the view and achievement that's my abiding memory of riding up Alpe d'Huez. It's Rog and his chaffed buttocks.

We spent the rest of the day riding up and down the climbs that surround this area. Each summit revealed another incredible view. At the top of one climb, we found a small B&B with a restaurant. They had a *plat du jour* of local beef cooked in red wine with a type of hand-made pasta. After riding for most of the day, we were starving and this sounded perfect. It also came with a starter, a salad comprising of smoked meat, cornichons, salad leaves and a poached egg with a mustard vinaigrette. For dessert, they had strawberry cheesecake.

The portions were huge. My lycra would have its work cut out if I ate all of it, which of course I did. We paid up and thanked the owner who, judging by the size of him, regularly enjoyed meals of this size, for breakfast lunch and dinner. He waved a *bon voyage* and we plummeted down the mountain like overweight lemmings.

Mark led the way and the rest of us followed behind. Each corner we took bit faster, going as quickly as we dared. I held back a bit. I've never been the bravest when it comes to descending (I much prefer going up hill). Besides, I'd spent enough time in hospital and as thankful as I am for everything they did, I didn't want to go back any day soon.

At the bottom of the hill, we saw a pro team unloading their bikes from their team van. Just before we got to them, Mark nearly came a cropper. His back wheel skidded out but luckily he managed to control it. He was going so fast, if he'd come off they wouldn't have needed a stretcher to pick him off the road, they'd have needed a spade.

As we went by, we could now see the team was Argos Shimano. One of the riders slowly shook his head at us. I wonder how many other amateurs they see on a daily basis riding around the Alps like idiots.

We were now back in the valley about 10km from the town of Borg D'oisans. We gave it full gas all the way back, riding flat out. Only the speed humps just outside the town slowed us down. Now drenched in sweat, we slowly pulled up by a small restaurant that was full of people eating. I'd pushed so hard I nearly saw the three-course dinner we'd eaten about an hour earlier. That would have been nice for diners sitting outside enjoying a cold glass of wine.

Riding in the Alps really is as good as it gets if you're into cycling. Commuting is probably the worst. Riding out into the British countryside can be great but being up in the mountains really is something else. It's the true spiritual home of cycling. There's nothing better.

Once back home I finished another month's worth of training, peaking two weeks before the race. I felt better than I'd ever done. I just had a couple of weeks to taper and then I'd be ready for race day. I was slightly nervous but excited, too. This would be the first race I'd done when my blood tests would be classed as 100 per cent healthy.

On Your Marks, Get Set, Stop

THE weather report for the race was terrible. Switzerland had had a really bad, long, cold winter, which had stretched into their summer. As we came into land, worryingly I could see the lush green fields below were all badly flooded.

The plane rocked from side to side as we got closer to the runway. We touched down with a thud and as we landed I noticed a windsock on the runway was sticking out at a right angle. It was incredibly windy, pouring with rain and as we got off the plane we felt how cold it was. Julie suggested we get back on the plane and go back home, where typically, the weather was glorious. At this present moment in time, this didn't sound like such a bad idea. But the optimist in me thought it might clear up in time for the race.

We cleared passport control and went outside. It was now raining sideways and it was freezing. Being out in this for a few minutes was unpleasant – never mind racing in it.

As I contemplated how miserable it would be to race in these conditions, a young Geordie guy came over and introduced himself as Dave, the rep from Nirvana travel. This was the first time I'd used Nirvana but now I use them for all my races. All you had to do was give them the dates of when you wanted to travel and they'd sort the rest. Bike transfer, hotel near the start, flights, airport pick-up. All you have to worry about is turning up at the airport on time.

As we drove through the torrential rain, Dave said he'd heard that they'd cancelled the swim because it was still far too cold. It was less than ten degrees, which even in a wetsuit would be freezing. I'd swam in really cold water before and it wasn't pleasant. In fact, it was so cold that I got cramp in my hands. It was horrible. I ended up swimming back to shore like a crab with arthritis.

I was gutted. I was coming here to beat my old 'sick' time. Now I couldn't compare. I sighed and looked out of the window at a river that had burst its banks. Dave went on to say that they were going to replace the swim with a 5km run. Great. So now I'd have to do my weakest discipline at the beginning and the end of the race. A 5km run, a 90km bike ride followed by another 21km run.

Despite the fact we were in the car for over 90 minutes, it rained constantly. The lake and the surrounding area looked stunning but the weather was doing its best to take the shine off the natural beauty of the place. I helped Dave unload my bike and went and checked into the hotel.

I felt sorry for Julie, too. If the weather was great, it would have actually been a nice break. But when the weather's this bad, there's not a lot you can do. She certainly wouldn't want to stand around and watch the race if the weather was like this.

I checked the weather forecast again on my phone – still terrible. I'm not sure what I was expecting. It didn't look like it was going to clear up any time soon. Once I'd unpacked everything, we went out to have a look around the town and find somewhere to eat. It was a quaint little place called Rapperswill Jona, which was situated on the upper end of lake Zurich.

The old town had quite a few restaurants and bars but because of the weather we didn't spend much time wandering around, so we went into the first place that looked half decent.

The menu didn't make much sense, so I asked the waiter to try and help. His English wasn't great and my German stretched to Vorsprung Durch Technik.

However, despite the fact that I was mono lingual, I thought I'd manage to order some kind of meaty pasta. But when it arrived, it turned out that through the confusion I'd ordered a huge lamb kebab. It was served on a pitta that could have doubled up as the sole of a shoe. We'd managed to find a Greek restaurant and not surprisingly for a Greek restaurant in Switzerland, it was terrible. I'm glad I wasn't racing tomorrow. Kebabs are rarely mentioned as the ultimate pre-race meal.

The following day, I woke up early to go the race meeting, rack my bike in transition and get my race number. Transition was flooded and as I trudged through the mud it took me back to my days at the Glastonbury Festival, except on this occasion I couldn't drown out the terrible weather with cheap cider.

The meeting was held in a sports centre. Everyone was dressed like it was the middle of winter. Until now, I'd been incredibly lucky with the weather but here my luck had run out quite spectacularly. They reinforced what I already knew. The swim was gone and it was to be replaced by the run. The bike sounded like it would have been great but the torrential rain that was forecast put a dampener on that.

I didn't mind running in the rain but this would mean there wouldn't be much support. That's one of the things I love about doing larger events, the support. But if the weather carried on like this, we'd be lucky to see anyone, except maybe a few Swiss ducks with nothing better to do on a rainy Saturday morning.

Despite all of this, I was still looking forward to racing. It was going to be a full stop on my recovery. If I could do this, I would have survived. In fact, I wouldn't have just survived, I'd have gone through all of it and come out the other side stronger.

I trudged back to the hotel in the pouring rain, ready to race. All I had to do was have a good nutritious meal and get some sleep. Who knows, maybe the weather would pick up a little. Let's face it, it couldn't get much worse.

I'd like to say I woke next morning to a warm, sunny day but this wasn't the case. It had actually stopped raining but the sky was still incredibly moody. It looked like it was only a matter if time before the heavens opened again.

I wasn't sure what to wear to race in, so I went with the 'too much is better than too little' approach. Luckily, the week before I'd brought a waterproof bike jacket, just in case the weather was bad. It wasn't very comfortable. It was like wearing a plastic bag but what it did have going for it was that it was completely waterproof.

We all gathered at the start ready for the first run. It looked dramatically different from the promotional pictures I'd seen on the website. But this is hardly surprising. A grey, cloudy, muddy field, filled with people wrapped up like they were going skiing, wouldn't have really sold it.

As we waited for the off, I noticed one of my fellow competitors had something written on his top in German about organ transplantation. As we've already established, my German is very limited but the German for organ transplant is *organtransplantation*. So even I could work out what this meant. I couldn't believe there was another transplant athlete racing. I asked him how long ago he'd had the operation but he smiled and said he hadn't. He was a surgeon from Hamburg and he was racing to raise money for his local hospital.

I told him about my condition and he congratulated me on my recovery. I shook his hand and wished him luck. It was a surgeon like him that who saved my life (although this didn't stop me from wanting to beat him).

The gun went off and I slowly jogged off around the 5km they'd put in place to replace the swim. About ten minutes in, it started to rain again. My trainers slowly filled with water and I continued to squelch around the course. Considering how bad the weather was, there was a surprising amount of people supporting.

I tried to keep my running steady. This was just the start after all. I was overtaken by quite a few people. Even though I hadn't raced in a while, I still remembered that it's best to hold back at the beginning and finish strong at the end. The first run was soon over and I waded into transition to put on my bike shoes, although wellies would have been more appropriate. The field was now so waterlogged that I didn't wheel my bike out, I carried it.

Out on the bike course, the rain started to get heavier and then the wind picked up. It was like the weather was having a competition to see how many people it could make pull out. I cycled on but it was getting seriously cold. The pouring rain and the wind were greatly reducing the temperature. I started to wonder what the hell I was doing. This was a million miles from how I imagined this race would go.

As I started to wonder how much more of this I could take before I went blue and froze to death, I noticed the pros were coming back down the road the other way. I knew they were considerably quicker than me but for them to be finishing the bike course already would have been impossibly quick. As they went past, I saw they weren't in the aero position but sitting up, chatting to each other. A couple of them were shaking their heads. Something was wrong.

They were followed closely behind by a two police motorbikes. One of the policeman had a passenger on the back who was waving his arms as if say 'cancelled'. I slowed down to try and ask some of the other riders what was going on. An English guy shouted: 'They've called off the race – there's been landslide.'

Part of me was relived because I was now freezing but another part of me, the bit of me that pushes me to do this kind of thing, was actually disappointed. We all slowly rode back to the start, stopping briefly at one of the aid stations to stuff as many gels into our pockets as we could. They were freely handing them out to anyone who stopped. With the race being cancelled, they'd have no use for them now.

We slowly regrouped in the sports centre, where they'd debrief us on what had happened. The first thing we were told was that we could transfer our entry to two other races. All we had to do was pay an extra 75 euros. Bargain, I sarcastically thought to myself. They could at least have given us free entry. But because I still had an itch that needed to be scratched, I knew I'd end up taking them up on the offer.

The guy on the stage then showed us a picture of the landslide. It looked pretty bad. It was right across the road. We were lucky no one was killed and it made sense for them to cancel the race. Everyone was gutted but it's not worth risking your life to race. He then told us that we'd done all the training and we'd started the race, so even if it was cancelled we should get our medals for getting this far.

I gladly accepted mine but it felt pretty hollow. I would have actually preferred it if they hadn't given any out. It should be something you can only get if you finish. But maybe this was a bit harsh. I briefly chatted to the guy next to me about how gutted I was not to race. He told me that he was particularly pissed off because he'd travelled form Australia. I suddenly felt much better about the situation.

I grabbed a few bottles of the free water and wandered off back to the hotel. The rain still didn't let up, so by the time I got back I was well and truly soaked. Julie was still asleep. As I crashed into the room with my bags and bike, she woke up with a start and looked up at me. 'What's happened?'

The expression on my face must have given away the fact that today had been a total wash-out. I explained what had happened and that she'd definitely made the right decision to stay in bed. I also tentatively told her about the option to race again in Germany. She said, well, it would be a shame to have done all that training and not get to race.

To soften the blow of another 'holiday' with my bike, I suggested we could fly out on Friday after work – I could register and rack my bike on Saturday – then race on Sunday and fly straight home. Surprisingly, Julie seemed more than up for the idea. This wouldn't be cheap but she could see how important it was to me. I got out of my wet clothes, had a shower and got into bed to go back to sleep. I'd been up since 4am and despite racing for less than 45 minutes, I was still knackered.

The Finish Line

WE landed at Frankfurt and our pilot did the usual speech about how grateful he was that we'd chosen his airline. This was followed by the good news that despite it being 7pm it was a clear night and the temperature was still a warm 20 degrees. This was no real surprise because after the weather in Switzerland I had checked the weather report on an hourly basis, every day, for the last two weeks. I even checked numerous websites to make doubly sure. For the last seven days, every website gave me the same news. Sun, sun, sun.

I picked up my bike from the oversized baggage area and went off to find the rep from Nirvana, who would drive us to the hotel. Just to be on the safe side, I asked him about the weather. He told us that it had been glorious and the forecast for the next few days was for this weather to continue. There was a chance the lake we were swimming in would be so warm that it might even be a no-wetsuit swim.

If my memory serves me correctly, anything over 24.5C would mean you couldn't wear a wetsuit. This didn't bother me massively but I knew it would mean my swim would be a lot slower. We arrived at the hotel, checked in and went upstairs to our room. I tentatively opened my bike box. I hated this part of the journey. A day before a race isn't the time to find out your bike has been turned into a very expense carbon jigsaw puzzle.

Thankfully, it had survived being treated like the losing wrestler in a particularly violent WWE bout, so it didn't take me long to put it back together. Once I'd got oil all over the floor, myself and the walls, we were ready to go out and get something to eat. After last time, I decided to ask reception if there was anywhere they could recommend. I asked if there were any restaurants that did nice, traditional German food. The receptionist laughed and said: 'Nice, traditional German food? Ha ha, our food is as well loved as our humour.'

While I admired his self-deprecating honesty, I was surprised he wasn't doing a little more to sell his country to me. He did say there was great local Italian down the road. An Italian guy had married a German woman about 20 years ago and they'd set up a restaurant and they were still working there today. He went on to tell me the man was the chef and the woman was head of the service. The passion for great food came from the Italian and the organisation and great service came from his German wife. What could be better, he said.

I had to agree that this sounded like a good set-up. Besides, Italian food would be a lot better for me than the kebab I'd managed to order last time. His recommendation didn't disappoint. The pasta was simple and delicious and the service was spot on. In fact, it was so good I booked a table for the following night, the night before the race.

The next morning, I had to get up and get a bus 30 minutes from the centre of town to the lake. Here, I would rack my bike then get the bus back again and set up my running stuff in the second transition area. This was the first race I'd done with a split transition. I thought it would be a bit of a mess but the organisation was second to none.

I arrived at the lake and it looked stunning. The clear blue water shimmered in the sunlight and it was just under the temperature that would mean wetsuits couldn't be used (phew). The water was fringed by high reeds and the entrance and the exit was out on to a golden sandy bank. It looked more like a place you'd visit on holiday than go to race. I had a good feeling about this.

I boarded the bus and went back into town. Loads of Ironman staff were out setting up barriers and the finish line was being put together. As I ambled around, I started to get butterflies.

The journey from discovering I was ill to dialysis through to the transplant was coming to an end. Finishing this race would be my final destination. It had been one hell of ride but I was now ready to get off.

The next day, my alarm went off at 5am and I tried to stop it before it woke Julie up. It was on the shelf above the bed. As I reached up to grab it, I dropped it down the back. By mistake the night before, I'd selected the cock crow alarm setting. This went off continually while I fumbled around in the dark trying to stop it. But I couldn't really see what I was doing. The sound of a cockerel crowing at this time of the morning was as welcome as the sound of a child scratching their nails down a blackboard.

I got up and tried to turn on the hotel room lights but rather than a light switch they had a digital control panel. Panicking, I stabbed at it trying to get my bedside light to come on but I turned on all the lights and the radio. Julie was now obviously wide awake.

I fumbled around under the bed trying to retrieve my phone. Finally, I reached it so I could turn it off. Then I went back to the control panel to try and turn off the radio (which was playing some kind of soft German rock). More prodding at the panel gave the desired result and I cut the band off mid-ballad. I also managed to dim the lights.

Julie was now totally awake and sitting up in bed. She said it would have been quieter to get a German Oompah band to wake me up with a live performance accompanied by a laser light show. I apologised and gathered all my bags together to go downstairs for breakfast. I kissed her goodbye and said I'd see her out on the run.

For breakfast, I had my usual bagel with banana and peanut butter, followed by a bowl of muesli. I also had a coffee, which was like rocket fuel. The spread of food was huge but I decided to give the large anaemic Bratwurst a miss. It looked more like something you'd buy in a sex shop than have for breakfast. This must have the style of food that the receptionist had been so complimentary about.

Phallic sausages aside, the rest of the food actually looked really good. I made up a couple of ham and cheese rolls. They were still warm, fresh from the bakers. I also snaffled a few pastries. This would give me something to eat after the race. They also had smoked salmon and Champagne (well, sparkling wine) but considering I was about to race for over (but hopefully under) six hours, I decided to give it a miss. Maybe later, I thought to myself.

I got on the bus and it was driven off towards the lake. There were athletes from all over the world. The guy sitting next to me was Spanish. There was a loud American couple at the back of the bus. There was an also an Australian and a group of Japanese guys. As we drove out of the city the sun started to rise, slowly burning away the grey mist. It looked like it was going to be a great day. It was also going to be tough. The bike course was incredibly hilly, with over 1,500m of climbing, but this was followed by an incredibly fast descent back into town, so my legs would have some respite before the run started.

The bus arrived and we all got off. I went over to find my bike to discover that my front tyre was flat. At first, I thought I had a puncture. But closer inspection revealed I'd forgotten to tighten the valve. Luckily, the race provided mechanics, who were all armed with track pumps, so this little problem didn't take long to remedy.

As I loaded my water bottles on to my bike, I noticed that a lot of the German athletes preferred the Speedo/crop top combo. This is what triathletes used to wear years ago. I'm guessing it all changed after one of them saw their reflection in the mirror. Add to this little outfit a cap and a moustache, and well, you get the picture. It looked like it was chucking out time at the Blue Oyster Bar. What I was wearing was pretty standard by comparison.

The announcer called out for all the people wearing green swim caps to come down to the lake. This was my age group, the 35-39-year-olds. We all nervously walked down towards the start. Everyone got into the water preparing themselves to be hit by the cold. But because it had been so warm, there was no deep breathing and swimming around to keep warm. It was more like getting into a warm bath.

We slowly paddled out to the start. The announcer reminded us that we had to do two lengths, with an Australian exit halfway through. This basically meant you swam 950 metres, came out of the water, ran out on to the beach, around a large inflatable, before running back into the lake to swim the distance again. Some people don't like this style of swim but I just saw it as a chance to give my arms a rest.

He also told us that it had remained a wetsuit swim by just .2 degrees, so those of us who weren't great swimmers had been saved by the smallest of margins. This was met with a cheer. He then counted down from ten. My swimming had improved, so I placed myself in the middle of the pack. Three, two, one and the horn sounded. Here we go again…

I felt pretty smooth in the water and I seemed to have chosen a good position. There was none of the usual jockeying for space. It was almost like I was swimming on my own. The sun was behind me, so I could easily pick off the buoys one at a time. This was a great start to the race. I was feeling strong and positive. In what seemed like no time, it was time to get out of the water, get out on to the beach and run round the yellow buoy for the second lap.

I thought I would start to get tired on the second lap but unlike the times before I felt great. This actually started to worry me a bit. Had I made a mistake and accidentally taken a shortcut? Well, it was too late now anyway. I crawled out of the water and ran up the bank to the area where we had to get changed out of our wetsuits. We had to stick it in a bag and drop it off on the way before we got on our bikes.

As I sat down, I looked down at my Garmin. My swim had taken me just over 33 minutes. I'd beaten my old time by three minutes. This spurred me on. Mark's kidney was doing me proud. In the excitement, I ran past the place where we were supposed to drop off our bags. Someone in the crowd shouted at me and pointed to where I should drop it. I ran back towards the drop-off point and hurled my bag towards it.

One of the stewards who was collecting the bags had bent down so I couldn't see them. They quickly stood back up and it hit them squarely in the face. Sorry – I shouted as I ran off to get on my bike. I looked back and thankfully they were smiling. They'd volunteered for this, they didn't get paid by anyone, so I'd have felt pretty bad if I'd taken one of them out.

I jumped on my bike and rode through the wooded area that surrounded the lake, out on to the open road. A 1,500m climb over 90km was going to be hard, so I made a mental note to go steady and not get carried away. We went through a small village and it looked like they'd all come out to support. There was a small incline, lined with locals with cow bells. My plan went straight out the window and I sprinted up it, spurred on by the local support.

I refocused and carried on with my race plan. The course was brutal. There was no let-up. The hills were long drags that slowly took everything out of you. But the views were incredible and I've never seen so many supporters. There were bands, schools, families and incredibly passionate locals who screamed at you as you went by. Despite how tiring it was, I couldn't help but smile.

Unlike my last 70.3 in the UK, I planned to eat a little and often. I'd set an alarm on my Garmin so I didn't forget. Someone once told me that the bike section of a long-distance triathlon should be approached like a rolling buffet. It's chance to fuel and digest plenty of food so you don't start the run on empty. It doesn't matter how good your 'engine' is, without any fuel you're going nowhere fast.

I came towards an aid station but I had plenty of food and drink, so I moved to the left of the road to go round it. Because a lot of people had been filling their water bottles, the road was wet and I nearly lost my front wheel as I turned on a drain cover. I quickly regained control. Christ, that was close.

The bike course continued to punish both my legs and my lungs. The sweat dripped from my forehead, down my face. I could taste the salt in it. I took an extra-long swig of my electrolyte drink and carried on. I looked down at my Garmin, which let me know I had 20km to go. The last 10km was down an incredibly steep hill that took us back into town. Not long now.

But the 10k to get there was all uphill again. The website described the bike course as 'interesting'. As I gasped for breath, stamping on the pedals and willing myself up the last climb, I could think of another word for it that would be more appropriate. Finally, I reached the top where the turning was. From here on, it was all downhill – thankfully only literally, not metaphorically.

I hunched down on my bike and got as aero as possible. I was easily hitting 75kph. I didn't dare take my eyes off the road for a second. I sped on. This fast finish would actually give me a respectable bike time considering how hard it had been. Soon, I was heading back to the town. The entire town had come out to watch and it looked like they'd invited all their friends, too. There were thousands of people there.

I swung around the last corner, jumped off my bike, handed it to one of the helpers who was there to rack it for me and slipped on my running shoes. A quick glance at my watch showed me I'd done the bike course in just under three hours 20 minutes. This wouldn't get me anywhere near qualifying for the world championships but it meant I was still on target to beat my old UK time. Plus, this was a much harder course.

I ran out of transition, off into the crowds that lined the route of the half-marathon. I was tired but even now I felt so much stronger than I had before. I thought back to the 10km I did while I was on dialysis. I was now running a whole minute per kilometre faster and this was after a swim and an incredibly lumpy bike. And all of this new found fitness was thanks to my brother, Mark. His donation had completely turned my life around. I owed him my life. I was so grateful.

At the halfway point, I noticed Julie. I ran over and gave her big sweaty kiss and a hug. 'Keep going, don't mind me,' she shouted. I ran back out on to the main loop. I had to do two more loops. Each time I ran round, I had to pick up another armband so the organisers knew that I'd done the full 21km and not missed one of the loops out, although there would be little point in doing this. The idea is to test yourself. For me, taking a shortcut would be completely pointless. I collected my third band, which signalled that I had just 5km to go. I upped my pace as much as I could but the bike course was now beginning take its toll. I actually felt strong but I had a sharp pain in my right leg. The faster I tried to go, the more it hurt. It wasn't the type of pain I could ignore.

Another check of my watch showed that I was still well on target to beat my old time, so I slowed and concentrated on finishing. The last thing I wanted now was to tear a muscle and pull out of the race. I ran passed the last aid station and took a couple gels. True to form, I managed to squirt one all over face but the other I swallowed before giving everything I had left, trying to make sure I didn't snap my calf like an old guitar string.

For the last 400m, I was like a man possessed. I sprinted flat out. What I hadn't taken into account was the finishing line photo. While others slowed and posed, I went flying over the line and ran into the fence in the finishers' pen. I hoped the finishing photographer had a fast shutter speed on his camera. As you can see from my finisher's photo in the middle of the book, my sprint finish didn't make for a great picture.

I looked down at my watch to see I'd beaten my old 70.3 time by around 16 minutes. This was my finish line in more ways than one. This is what I'd wanted for so long, to feel fit and healthy again. Just before I let my emotions get the better of me, I decided to go and find Julie. She gave me a big hug, then recoiled as she realised I was covered in sweat and energy gels.

I went into the town hall next to the finishers' area to collect the print-out of my official time.

> Swim: 0:33:09
> Bike: 3:19:31
> Run: 1:56:56

I had a PB in the swim but not the bike – which wasn't surprising considering how hard it was – and a PB on the run. All in all, it had been a great race. As I walked out of the town hall, the euphoria began to wear off and my legs started to stiffen. I looked around to see I was surrounded by men in Speedos and crop tops. It was time to get out of here and pick up all my stuff, including my bike, from transition and get something to eat at the hotel.

As I walked into the hotel, a group of people clapped me as I walked into reception. I looked around assuming this was for someone else. But they were clapping me, which was a bit weird. But I thanked them and smiled, before slowly staggering off upstairs to get some rest.

The End

SINCE finishing this race, I've raced half Ironmans in Mallorca, Austria St Polten, Austria Zell Am See and just last month I set a new PB while racing in Budapest, with a time of 5hrs 23mins. What started as something to keep me fit has now become a big part of my life. My doctors agree that my training and focus helped me massively, from my diagnosis, through both types of dialysis, up to my operation and out the other side.

My fitness has made a huge difference to how I dealt with this whole ordeal. One day, I'll do the full distance again but not just yet. At the minute, I'm just happy to be back to being 100 per cent healthy.

I've also been lucky enough to bear witness to the toughest endurance 'event' on the planet, when Julie gave birth to our first child.

Our daughter, Maisie, was born at 6.14pm, weighing 7lbs 8oz, on 5 September 2015. She was born ten days late via C-section after Julie went through 36 hours of labour. Watching Julie go through this for what seemed like days, before having a caesarean, certainly put my achievements in the shade. This made triathlon look like a walk in the park.

Writing this has confirmed a lot of things that I already knew but putting them into words has made me realise just how lucky I am. There are thousands of people out there waiting for a transplant.

But I was lucky to have an incredible brother who was prepared to make a huge sacrifice for me.

I was lucky that my body accepted it.

And I am lucky that, four years later, it's still going strong.

However, there are thousands who aren't.

So it's my hope that everyone who reads this goes on to register to be organ donor because I'm living proof that organ donation really does totally change people's lives for the better.

The many people I've relayed my story to have described it in various ways. People have said brave, inspirational, and someone even rather embarrassingly referred to me as heroic.

But there's only one real hero in this story.

And that's my brother.

My brother Mark.

To register as an organ donor visit:
www.organdonation.nhs.uk/register-to-donate
